TWO ONE PONY

The Stackpole Military History Series

**THE AMERICAN
CIVIL WAR**

Cavalry Raids of the Civil War
Ghost, Thunderbolt, and Wizard
In the Lion's Mouth
Pickett's Charge
Witness to Gettysburg

WORLD WAR I

Doughboy War

WORLD WAR II

After D-Day
Airborne Combat
Armor Battles of the Waffen-SS,
    1943–45
Armoured Guardsmen
Army of the West
Arnhem 1944
Australian Commandos
The B-24 in China
Backwater War
The Battle of France
The Battle of Sicily
Battle of the Bulge, Vol. 1
Battle of the Bulge, Vol. 2
Beyond the Beachhead
Beyond Stalingrad
The Black Bull
Blitzkrieg Unleashed
Blossoming Silk against the
    Rising Sun
Bodenplatte
The Brandenburger Commandos
The Brigade
Bringing the Thunder
The Canadian Army and the
    Normandy Campaign
Coast Watching in World War II
Colossal Cracks
Condor
A Dangerous Assignment
D-Day Bombers
D-Day Deception
D-Day to Berlin
Destination Normandy
Dive Bomber!
A Drop Too Many
Eagles of the Third Reich
The Early Battles of Eighth Army
Eastern Front Combat
Europe in Flames
Exit Rommel
The Face of Courage
Fist from the Sky
Flying American Combat Aircraft
    of World War II
For Europe
Forging the Thunderbolt
For the Homeland
Fortress France

The German Defeat in the East,
    1944–45
German Order of Battle, Vol. 1
German Order of Battle, Vol. 2
German Order of Battle, Vol. 3
The Germans in Normandy
Germany's Panzer Arm
    in World War II
GI Ingenuity
Goodwood
The Great Ships
Grenadiers
Guns against the Reich
Hitler's Nemesis
Hold the Westwall
Infantry Aces
In the Fire of the Eastern Front
Iron Arm
Iron Knights
Japanese Army Fighter Aces
JG 26 Luftwaffe Fighter Squadron
    War Diary, Vol. 1
Kampfgruppe Peiper at the Battle
    of the Bulge
The Key to the Bulge
Knight's Cross Panzers
Kursk
Luftwaffe Aces
Luftwaffe Fighter Ace
Luftwaffe Fighter-Bombers
    over Britain
Luftwaffe Fighters and Bombers
Massacre at Tobruk
Mechanized Juggernaut or
    Military Anachronism?
Messerschmitts over Sicily
Michael Wittmann, Vol. 1
Michael Wittmann, Vol. 2
Mountain Warriors
The Nazi Rocketeers
Night Flyer / Mosquito Pathfinder
No Holding Back
On the Canal
Operation Mercury
Packs On!
Panzer Aces
Panzer Aces II
Panzer Aces III
Panzer Commanders of the
    Western Front
Panzergrenadier Aces
Panzer Gunner
The Panzer Legions
Panzers in Normandy
Panzers in Winter
Panzer Wedge
The Path to Blitzkrieg
Penalty Strike
Poland Betrayed
Red Road from Stalingrad
Red Star under the Baltic

Retreat to the Reich
Rommel's Desert Commanders
Rommel's Desert War
Rommel's Lieutenants
The Savage Sky
Ship-Busters
The Siege of Küstrin
The Siegfried Line
A Soldier in the Cockpit
Soviet Blitzkrieg
Stalin's Keys to Victory
Surviving Bataan and Beyond
T-34 in Action
Tank Tactics
Tigers in the Mud
Triumphant Fox
The 12th SS, Vol. 1
The 12th SS, Vol. 2
Twilight of the Gods
Typhoon Attack
The War against Rommel's
    Supply Lines
War in the Aegean
War of the White Death
Winter Storm
Wolfpack Warriors
Zhukov at the Oder

**THE COLD WAR /
VIETNAM**

Cyclops in the Jungle
Expendable Warriors
Fighting in Vietnam
Flying American Combat Aircraft:
    The Cold War
Here There Are Tigers
Land with No Sun
MiGs over North Vietnam
Phantom Reflections
Street without Joy
Through the Valley
Two One Pony

**WARS OF AFRICA AND
THE MIDDLE EAST**

Never-Ending Conflict
The Rhodesian War

**GENERAL MILITARY
HISTORY**

Carriers in Combat
Cavalry from Hoof to Track
Desert Battles
Guerrilla Warfare
Ranger Dawn
Sieges
The Spartan Army

TWO ONE PONY

An American Soldier's Year in Vietnam, 1969

Charles R. Carr

STACKPOLE
BOOKS

Published by
STACKPOLE BOOKS
5067 Ritter Road
Mechanicsburg, PA 17055
www.stackpolebooks.com

Cover design by Tracy Patterson

Printed in the United States of America

10 9 8 7 6 5 4 3 2 1

Library of Congress Cataloging-in-Publication Data

Carr, Charles R., 1945–
  Two one pony : an American soldier's year in Vietnam, 1969 / Charles R.
Carr.
      p. cm. — (Stackpole military history series)
    ISBN 978-0-8117-0733-6
  1. Carr, Charles R., 1945– 2. Vietnam War, 1961–1975—Personal narratives, American. 3. United States. Army. Infantry Regiment, 47th. Battalion,
2nd 4. United States. Army—Officers—Biography. 5. Soldiers—United
States—Biography. I. Title. II. Title: American soldier's year in Vietnam,
1969.
  DS559.5C385 2012
  959.704'342—dc23
                              2011036268

Contents

Prologue

For the army, a tour of duty in Vietnam was one year. Someone had determined that properly prepared soldiers, after a couple of months' experience in the field, and backed with an overwhelming firepower advantage, could be a significant presence for the remaining part of the year without degrading support for the war at home the way an indefinite tour might.

The one-year tour came to be seen differently by those fighting the war. For many a draftee, the object then became simply to stay alive for a year. Those who made it into their eighth or ninth or tenth month began to think they might survive. At the point where they would be expected to understand something of how to fight the war, their thoughts were focused on surviving it. Someone who woke up thinking he had only eighty days left was not what advanced infantry training had projected. The goal for many became surviving their year. In some strange, looping circle it became its own goal: we were here for a year to survive for a year, but with no idea of how to understand the length of a year. You had been here a month or two months. Eleven months to go did not seem particularly different from twelve. That was still forever.

The tour for company-grade officers—lieutenants and captains—justified and reinforced the one-year focus for enlisted personnel. Normally, junior officers spent part of their year in a command position in the field and part in a staff position, working, for example, in intelligence or operations or personnel. No matter how the army tried to justify it, the implications were obvious to those at the bottom: winning this war was less important that giving "valuable career experience" to officers. Why put yourself at risk for an officer who wasn't going to be there in a few months, who instead would be in an operations bunker or a personnel office, going to the officers' club every night?

And you entered the war alone. Those you knew from training and reencountered for a day or two at Long Binh Replacement were scattered across half a dozen different divisions. Those united for a week at the division's school were scattered across its three brigades. Those sent to the same battalion were apportioned to companies and platoons based on their needs. All you shared with those with whom you arrived was the DEROS, the Date of Estimated Return from Over Seas.

Even in the first few months when a year was an inconceivable amount of time, the year continued to be the one thought that conditioned everything else. Someone's making it out alive, surviving his year, only reminded you of the time you had left—eight months, ten months, eleven months. You couldn't be happy for them without at the same time resenting their departure, leaving you here to carry on without them. Anger and resentment, and then guilt about feeling angry and resentful, were constant companions.

All of this, no matter how one felt about the rightness of the cause. Some, no doubt, were saints who didn't feel the negative emotions or heroes who carried on unaffected by them. Most of us were neither.

The North Vietnamese teenagers just kept walking down the trail with that damn tattoo, "Born in the North to Die in the South." Back home, the antiwar movement was reluctant to admit there were North Vietnamese fighting in the South, insisting that this war was a revolt by indigenous South Vietnamese. The Right had us fighting global communism, with Cambodia and Thailand the next two dominoes, standing only so long as South Vietnam did. While we died, the political groups would not acknowledge facts that did not support their ideology. The Right and the Left made the question of whom we were fighting sound like a commercial: *"It's a local insurgency. It's an international communist conspiracy. It's a candy mint. It's a breath mint."*

CHAPTER 1

Arrival—May 1969

We were drifting in and out of conversations about a world now twenty hours behind us, conversations constructed from too little sleep and too much adrenaline, when the last part of the pilot's announcement riveted everyone's attention to a single present: "Due to vectors of artillery fire, we will be altering course for arrival in Saigon."

We gasped, laughing the same nervous laugh. We listened as fifty conversations fell silent. Thousands of feet below us was the war. All too soon, it would be our war and some plane would be altering course for us, dispelling the thoughts and conversations that were its momentary cargo.

With the pilot's words, I felt the fading of any remaining hope that something would somehow rescue me. I was here. None of the miracles that were going to prevent the arrival of this moment had intervened. No sudden peace treaty. No last-minute assignment elsewhere.

Time itself had failed. In early 1966, I drove to Boulder with three friends to attend a teach-in on the war. Three years later, there is still a war. People are still killing and being killed while, back in the world, helpless families are attached to TV screens for any word that might tell them someone was all right for another day.

Vectors of artillery fire.

The plane landed. We stepped off into the Vietnamese sun. A few dazed first steps on Vietnamese soil and then slowly we began to focus on the cheering that rolled through rows of soldiers in dirty, faded fatigues and worn jungle boots, soldiers who stared not so much at us as through us. The cheer would start to ebb and then pick up again, as if they could not let go

1

of it. Its meaning, hidden beneath a year in-country, eluded us. In a year, perhaps the fortunate among us would find ourselves cheering as frightened kids in new fatigues stepped off a plane and walked through our stares. They would stare back, a year removed from the meaning of their own first minutes.

Three other fragments stood out in the confusion and drama of those first minutes. Heat. Suffocating heat. Heat that made the air feel heavy. Wire mesh. Wire mesh was everywhere. It was in the windows of the buses we boarded. Wire mesh to stop the hand grenade that might try to find its way on board. Grasping at straws. I grasped. I looked through the mesh-guarded windows at the Vietnamese we passed. They looked different. They dressed differently. Maybe that was the good part about being here: exposure to a different culture, a different people. That would make me better for having been here. I tried desperately to believe it.

Military transfer stations like the Long Binh Replacement Detachment a few miles northeast of Saigon, where the bus with the wire-mesh windows delivered us and where we would await our permanent assignments, are not intended to make life comfortable for those who pass through. Nobody should want to linger. Getting to your unit should be a relief. So while you are there, you are given work to do. You pick up trash or clean an office or cut weeds or mark the borders of walkways by lining up rocks. "Details," the military calls them. You are on litter detail or ditch-digging detail or rock-placing detail. At a transfer station, it is not so much work that must be done as work that will keep everyone busy.

I suspected the first formation was a detail formation to occupy us while our records were processed. I thought about moving to a more inconspicuous part of the formation, but concluded there was little chance someone wouldn't notice. I just waited for someone to tell me where to go and what to do once I got there.

I had learned the lesson in basic training. Don't stand out. Don't volunteer anything—even information. It was early somewhere in my first weeks in the army. A private first class brought a folder to the sergeant who had just finished his lecture. The sergeant appeared to read a paper from the file and then asked if there were any college graduates in the room. At last! The fact I didn't belong here with the rest of these people had finally been recognized. Along with two others, I bit. I raised my hand. The smiles told me immediately I had made a mistake. They took us to their office and told us to get busy. They needed someone to clean their office, and we had just volunteered. They stood in the doorway grinning at each other as we swept the floor, emptied trash, and wiped out ashtrays. They had ambushed some college boys.

But I had paid attention in all those classes. "Take the offensive," instructor after instructor had said. "You have a better chance of surviving an ambush if you attack it."

With the two instructors distracted and engaged in a premature victory celebration, I practiced what I had learned about taking the offensive and emptied the ashtrays I was cleaning into the pockets of the jackets hanging in their office. On a training base, cadre never put their hands in their pockets—not the military bearing the army wants to provide the trainees. It would be a while, days or perhaps weeks, before they found the contents of the ash trays in their pockets, learned their ambush of the college kids had failed, and realized they had lost this fight. They might win the war and turn me into a soldier, but not without cost. Not without losing a few battles. I glanced at the window of their office as we marched away from the classroom, and as much as I hated admitting it, the drill sergeant had been right. There would be times when you had gotten payback on the enemy and really get off on war.

On this first day of the real war, the "Be Quiet and Wait to Be Selected Strategy" appeared to have worked. There were fewer work assignments than there were people in formation. Seemingly at random, they had taken three from one place in formation, two from another. When they ran out of work assignments, I was one of six still standing. The person in charge looked at us, paused a moment, warned us against leaving this company area, and told us to report back at 1300 hours for the next formation. One free morning.

I didn't get a chance to try the strategy again. At the next formation, they read more assignments. My name was on a manifest with fifteen or twenty others for the 9th Infantry Division—the "Flower Power" division, the officer-in-charge called it as he read off our names. One of the fifteen was not like the rest of us. He already had the 9th Division's insignia, the Octo-foil, on his sleeve. He was returning to his unit after spending two weeks recovering from wounds. We gathered around him.

Someone asked, "What is it like in the 9th Division? Much action?"

"Where is it?" asked another.

The questions were the questions of those new to the country, new guys, of FNGs who didn't yet know what it meant to be a new guy. Our questions didn't merit answers. We would not understand. We got only the briefest response from him, spoken in words of the same secret language that so many spoke here. Speaking in the language of private words and unnatural rhythms that we would find ourselves speaking, he whispered, "Watch out for Charles. Charles will DEROS you."

CHAPTER 2

Dong Tam

The 9th Division was the southernmost American ground combat division in Vietnam, with an area of responsibility stretching from Long An Province south of Saigon well into the northern Mekong Delta. It extended to the west into the Plain of Reeds, adjacent to North Vietnamese bases in Cambodia. I knew only that we were flying south. From the air, it was spectacular country. But amidst the beauty, there were always the reminders of where we were and why: craters from artillery shells and bombs marked the countryside, endless miles of a bad teenage complexion.

We landed at the division base camp at Dong Tam, several hundred acres dredged from the mud of the My Tho River, the northern arm of the Mekong. "Welcome to the 'Nam." The young sergeant didn't have time to finish his welcoming speech. "Drop everything and follow me," he ordered as he sprinted to an above-ground bunker. As we ran, we picked up the sound of explosions in the background. Voices shouted, "Incoming." A distant siren joined the chorus. We ran out of the sun and into the darkness of the bunker, where we sucked in the heavy, black air. Only the occasional flash of a Zippo lighting a cigarette broke the darkness.

"Just Victor Charlie welcoming you to Dong Tam," the sergeant's voice explained. "Usually doesn't happen that often during the day." He may have sensed that we still didn't know what had happened and patiently connected the dots for us. "Local VC saw your plane land and took the opportunity to fire a few mortar rounds into the camp. Just harassment. They hit us, mostly mortars, two or three times each night, thinking it will disrupt our sleep and keep us edgy. And maybe when we're out, we will be a bit too tired. Won't see that booby trap that with another hour of sleep we might have. They can't overrun this base, but when they want to, they can really bring smoke. Couple of months back, they hit the ammo dump with a 122-millimeter rocket. All the ammo for the 9th Division. When something like that happens, you don't *even* want to be here."

There it was again. Everybody stressing the word "even" to create an emphatic adverb. It sounded too unnatural, too forced. Some of the new guys had already picked it up, trying to sound like they belonged. "Not me," I thought. "I'm not *even* going to talk that way."

A siren wailed in the distance, and down the line came the calls of "All clear." We stumbled back to where we had dropped our duffel bags as our eyes readjusted to the Vietnamese sun.

"Welcome to 'Nam," the processing sergeant began again, unruffled by the attack. "You're here now. Long Binh. Binh Hoa. They ain't Vietnam. Nothing but clerks and MPs and their round-eyed boom-boom. No! Boom-boom ain't the explosions we just heard. You'll be here five days. You'll write a letter home, get your rifle and sight it, fill out a bunch of damn paper for the damn clerks to put in their damn files, and then spend a few days at our charm school. The staff at the school will try to teach you what war in the Delta is like. It ain't like nowhere else. Pay attention. It might get you home alive. One more thing. Unless you are with the staff at the school, don't leave the training area here. Some of the rest of the base belongs to line companies, and grunts don't like new guys who haven't earned the right in their areas. You ain't earned it."

Joined by others who had arrived the previous day, we spent the afternoon with various work details. Two of us went off with a sniper to be put to work cleaning the snipers' hootch. "Hootch," we learned, was the term of choice for a soldier's sleeping quarters or for small rural Vietnamese dwellings. He gave us a beer and told us to sweep out the rooms and then look busy whenever anyone came around.

We asked, "What is it like?" hoping to get some sense of what awaited us. But like the wounded soldier at the replacement station, he declined to answer the questions. It seemed everyone guarded some secret we were to discover ourselves. We were monks among zen masters still unsure if they really had a secret to reveal or if it was all a game that only they understood. I had to know more. I changed the subject and asked him about his weapon, the sniper's rifle he had taken apart while we played at work. "Why not the M16 that everyone trained on for Vietnam?"

"Snipers don't *even* get close to what they're shooting at," he explained. "We need something accurate at distance. We're about the only ones here who see what we blow away. You will never see who you kill or who kills you. Mostly, it will just happen."

Not capital-T truth, but I thought I had gotten my first answer. The first piece of the puzzle? Would the gods of war expect payment for my presumption? I took the afternoon of cleaning seriously. I owed him that. I feared I owed the war gods more.

The explosions which had greeted us earlier that day rocked the Delta night. I stepped out of a restless sleep and into unlaced jungle boots, running after the voices that seemed to know where they were going—this time out of the dark night into a darker bunker. We huddled together as people kept pouring in. Acknowledgments of "Incoming" and "Outgoing" or "Close" were attached by those around me to the—for me—indistinguishable sounds.

In the dark, no one could tell if the one-word lectures were being conducted by those who knew what they were talking about. They could be the words of those who, not three days ago, were waiting to board a plane in Oakland. Or maybe everyone had already picked up the signatures of sounds that still eluded me. I did not know how large the bunker protecting me was or how secure it was. I did not know if this was the bunker. I turned to what I assumed would put me face to face with someone. A smaller explosion was heard, coupled with smaller amounts of dust and sawdust settling on us.

I spoke to the man in front of me. "Any idea how of how far off that last one hit?"

"Hundred-plus meters," he said. "Maybe outside the company area completely. That first one, though, was no more than about half of that."

He sounded like he knew what he was talking about, so I asked him about the large above-ground bunkers. "Wouldn't have to dig too much, and we'd all be sitting in the water. Notice the chain-link fencing circling the bunker. Hope is that they'll set the shaped charge from a rocket or RPG early." He noted that it sounded about over. "More than a couple of minutes and we have the trajectory of their incoming and know where they're firing from and can return it."

Fear fought its way out. Less than one day and I had been mortared twice. This was a division base camp. What would it be like in the field? Hell, would I even make it to the field? I managed to stop myself and sat thinking about nothing.

Eventually, only "Outgoing" followed the distant roars until "All clear" echoed across the night. I had run only a hundred meters from the bunk to the bunker, but in the night, I was lost. There was a lesson to learn here, but I was too numb to think clearly. I looked for someone familiar to follow back to the barracks.

They say not to think about how much time you had left. It only made it pass more slowly. But I couldn't help it as I glanced at my watch, noting it was after midnight. Date of Estimated Return from Overseas: 362 days and a wake-up.

The five days of division training prepared us for very little. Like stateside Basic and Advanced Individual Training, it was designed to get a lot of men through fast. In groups, we walked through mock jungle with mock booby traps. The first person in line saw something or he didn't. If he didn't, he tripped a smoke grenade. Instructors were quickly in their faces screaming, "You're dead. You're dead because you weren't paying attention." Then the second person in line took over until a smoke grenade "killed" him. Those in the back half of the column just stepped over the wires pointed out to them by men in front. At the end, they dutifully yelled at us about how we were all going to get ourselves killed if we didn't learn to pay attention, about what percentage of the 9th Division's casualties were from booby traps or rifle fire or rocket fire. No one cared enough to walk us through one at a time, showing us what we missed, letting everyone hear the barely audible scrape of the wire pulling the pin from the grenade.

A few weeks earlier, in infantry training at Fort Lewis, four of us were accidentally left behind one morning on a training exercise. Our training company was in the forests of Washington for a week of being ambushed, setting up night defensive positions, and attacking enemy positions. "Viet Cong" patrols wandered the jungles of Fort Lewis, setting those ambushes and assaulting those who tried for a few hours of sleep. That morning, either intending realism or just to give those who didn't look too busy something to do while the company prepared to move out, several of us were sent out from the perimeter to serve as a listening post while the company waited for its day to start. We didn't know what a listening post was, so we listened. Over our shoulders, we listened to the company move out. Nobody came to get us. Not knowing whether we had been forgotten or whether this was part of the training, we waited and listened some more. Half an hour passed. Nobody came. Finally, we set out after the company that we now realized had forgotten us.

For a day, we were on our own, training ourselves as we tried to find our company without being taken prisoner by marauding VC. From hideaways, we watched training platoons walk into ambushes. Hidden in rocks high above a field, we watched ambushed convoys assault the ambush, each assault lasting twenty minutes. Only later—when people hidden above the battle not in rocks but in helicopters would tell me what I could do—would it strike me how, from such heights, battles appear so much more organized and less violent than they really are. Had Robert E. Lee been a thousand meters above the battle, how much less terrible might he have found it.

Later that morning, as we walked along the edge of a road, a group spotted us and, thinking we were part of their training exercise, gave chase. We eluded them easily by melting thirty feet into the wood line. I learned more that day than I learned the rest of the week—about how quickly people could disappear into the jungle, about how noisy American soldiers are, about how easy it is to become separated from your unit, about how much advantage those who know the terrain even moderately have, and about much you rely on other people. It was my best day of training.

We found the company that afternoon. A captain screamed about discipline and Article 15s, an administrative punishment, for avoiding training. I tried to explain that he overestimated us, that we couldn't have planned to wander around for a day, but someone, emboldened by the day's survival, interrupted. "No, sir! It will have to be a court martial where you will get to explain how you lost half of a squad for most of a day and didn't know it." We hadn't eaten all day, and to save face, he sent us back to our platoon without letting us eat. The next day, our company was ambushed and then attacked an enemy position across from some rocks that overlooked the battlefield. The victory took twenty minutes. The rumor in the company was that one of the lost guys from the day before had won $50 betting on details of the day's action. It was closer to $20.

The rest of the week at Dong Tam, we pulled guard duty at night in bunkers where the several-hundred-meter-wide My Tho River formed one perimeter. During the day, we walked through mock jungle not seeing mock bunkers. We attached trip wires to flares. We learned again about radio protocols and reading map coordinates and calling in artillery. We learned about enemy sappers who could crawl through wire and into our bunkers without our knowing they'd been there. We learned not to put twenty rounds in our twenty-round magazines because the M16 would jam if we did. At every moment, we learned about the heat, heat that never broke, that greeted us early in the morning, that woke us several times every night as if to remind us how dangerous sleeping was.

We got out of the sun only when they tried to convince those of us with the right aptitude scores to sign up for officer candidate school or helicopter flight school. The last chance to avoid being an enlisted grunt, and all it would cost was one extra year of active duty in the army. I didn't understand the calculus that would solve the equation: chance of being killed in the infantry minus the chance of being killed flying a helicopter plus the cost of one additional year in the army. Some traded away their year. I didn't.

Those directly in charge of our training at Dong Tam were also war profiteers. In the afternoons, they would sell us cold Cokes at inflated prices, and we were grateful to them for the one part of the day we looked forward to, a few minutes of something cold. When they couldn't get the Cokes to us, we were angry at those, the officers and senior NCOs, who would stop their enterprise.

Finally, they gave us one last chance to trade a year for the promise of something better. Then they sent us to fight the war.

CHAPTER 3

First Mission

I looked back at Dong Tam from the back of a mail truck bound for the 2nd Battalion, 47th Infantry, at Binh Phuoc in Long An Province. "You'll be riding ponies," the driver had said matter-of-factly, as though we should understand. The ride to Binh Phuoc provided a closer look at the terrain viewed earlier from the air and a first look at the enemy. On both sides of the two-lane road, rice paddies were laced with dikes that made an efficient walkway through the fields when the rain filled the paddies. The nipa palm jungles grew along either side of the rivers and canals that traced paths through the larger countryside just as the dikes traced paths through individual rice paddies. Men in black shorts and conical hats continued working in paddies, not pausing to look up as we passed. When we got off the blacktop and onto dirt roads, even the dust the truck kicked up did not draw their acknowledgment.

At the end of the ride, I was processed into Alpha Company, 2nd Battalion, 47th Infantry (Mechanized), where I made sure everyone knew about my secondary Military Occupational Specialty, clerk-typist. This was, I was sure, no time for subtlety or to yield to a basic shyness. Subtle or not, my primary MOS was infantry. A boonie-humping grunt, I was assigned to the 2nd Platoon, 1st Squad. The pony I would ride was that squad's armored personnel carrier, *Two One Pony*.

The 2nd of the 47th at Binh Phuoc occupied a rectangular-shaped base camp, approximately 125 meters across and perhaps 400 in length. An artillery battery occupied one corner of the base, and a 4.2-inch mortar platoon was located near the center. There was a large maintenance area for the armored

personnel carriers just inside the front gate. Binh Phuoc was
the home of three mechanized infantry companies and one
scout platoon. It also housed the maintenance and combat
support company. Near the center of the camp was the battalion headquarters. Two-story wooden bunkers guarded the
perimeter just inside a cyclone fence that circled the camp.
Outside the fencing was row after row of razor concertina wire.
All in all, the camp was home to perhaps 800 soldiers, out of
the 543,000 that currently marked American troop strength in
Vietnam at its highest point of the war.

The company clerk took me to find the squad, noting,
"The company got back from the field earlier today. Some will
be in the enlisted club. Lot of guys go there to write letters."

"What about life on armored personnel carriers?" I asked,
not sure what I was asking. "How different is it than regular
infantry?"

He explained thoroughly, "Not at all, really."

"Nothing?"

"You're still in the infantry. The armored personnel carriers—everyone calls them 'tracks' because of the tracked
wheels—just take you to where you get off and hump the paddies. Once you're there, you walk in the sun like everyone else.
Same-same with the riverines down on their boats. Boats,
tracks, trucks, or helicopters. Don't *even* mean nothing. They're
all just infantry delivery systems. Tracks make the most noise,
though. They'll hear you coming. No fighting unless they want
to, is what it means."

He found some members of the 2nd Platoon in the enlisted
men's club, introduced me, and then quickly departed as if he
didn't belong there. Benny, who carried the squad's machine
gun, looked every bit the surfer incarnated from a Beach Boys
song. Blond hair too long for the army swept across his forehead. Next to me, he was the newest guy in the squad. The
track driver, like many with special roles, was known by that job
and as often as not was simply "Driver." From appearance and
manner, he could have been one of the inmates from the high
school metal shop class I signed up for as a sophomore, naively

thinking it was a real class in which I might learn to do something with my hands. I spent the year negotiating deals to keep from being welded to a table. Driver could have been their leader.

Donald was tall and thin and had been in country for four months. His height partially disguised how young he looked.

Two more from the platoon walked in together and moved to our table. One was from the 1st Squad. Rick provided the New Jersey accent that no war movie could be without. Mike looked like he could have been a linebacker. Although he was assigned to another squad, Mike seemed to transcend that "assigned somewhere" quality of military existence. Sunglasses pushed up onto his forehead, he went into one of the speeches that provided his identity within the platoon, "Audie Murphy." He took a seat and then turned to the others at the table. "A lot of walking out there today, men. Walking with no discernible purpose. Lesser men might complain, but not me. I did it for my country." Then returning to normal voice, "Anybody got some paper I can borrow?"

New arrivals to the club were asked if they had seen Robe the Strobe. Someone gave me a pen and a couple of sheets of paper. With nothing to say, I still joined the letter-writing frenzy, which continued until someone pronounced it time to eat. I followed them to the mess hall and, afterward, to the artillery area, where they decided the night's movie wasn't worth seeing.

As darkness took charge, we walked to the motor pool for my first look at *Two One Pony*. Tracks weigh about twelve tons and have armor that will stop rifle fire and explosive fragmentation from penetrating. But the armor does not stop the rocket-propelled grenades (RPG) that every Viet Cong or North Vietnamese Army squad carries as part of its normal load.

"Anyone riding inside is dead if an RPG round hits," Rick explained in his very matter-of-fact manner. "So everyone rides on top. You'll get blown off the top and break whatever you land on. Better than being inside. Much better."

Two One Pony was dirtier than the armored personnel carriers we had ridden once during basic training. Outside, mud and dust caked everything. Inside, rations, Coke, and beer shared space with boxed ammunition. Two hammocks were tied to the walls inside. On top of the track, surrounded by an inch-thick steel cupola, sat a .50-caliber machine gun. I had fired the .50 in training, remembering the small trees it cut down. More canisters of ammunition were scattered on top of the track for easy access

"It's home," Donald said. "We have no barracks, no hootch, no bunker. When we are in camp, those with cots usually sleep under the corrugated metal roof that covers part of the motor pool shop. Unless the rain comes in from the south, they're dry."

Until I was able to steal a cot, or someone left and I inherited one, it was best, I was told, to sleep on top of the track when we were in camp. I would be off the ground and away from the rats.

Sitting under the roof of the motor pool shop, they began asking me polite questions about myself, designed not to elicit too much information. It was in the field that I would either prove myself or fail. I gave them the limited information they wanted. I grew up in Colorado. I was drafted out of graduate school. I'd had two years of ROTC in college and genuinely hated every minute of it. And finally and reluctantly, I had been a philosophy major. The reaction I waited for—the jokes about "real" bullets—never came.

Then they began to talk, and the information overload began.

"Usually, the platoon's out for two or three days and in for an overnight to give everyone's feet a chance to dry out. Jungle rot! Gotta let the feet dry out."

"Since we came in early today, we probably move out early tomorrow, but since Doug, the squad leader, hasn't said anything yet, maybe we'll have another day standing down. In the mud around the canals, they could hide almost anything.

Booby traps you'll never see. There, everyone wants Doug walking point. He sees everything."

"Every seventh mission or so, you stay with the tracks pulling guard or manning a listening post instead of humping the paddies."

"The battalion base camp where we now are sitting was last under ground attack in February when several members of the scout platoon were killed when a rocket destroyed their hootch. One of the mechanized companies just happened to be returning to Binh Phuoc then, and caught the bad guys in the open."

Since about January, there had been a lot of contact in the area, but that had apparently slowed down starting about two weeks ago.

They pronounced our Hispanic platoon leader, Two Six, "pretty cool for an officer." On missions, he rode with the squad on *Two One Pony*. "Six" identified his role as a commander, as a leader. As the platoon leader for the 2nd Platoon, he was "Two Six" or, if his company needed to be identified, he was Alpha Two Six. The commander of Alpha Company was "Alpha Six."

Our squad leader, Doug, I had figured out, was "Robe the Strobe" and "Robey" and "Robe." He answered to any variant.

Benny noted we were doing well. Nobody had been killed in the squad since February when a brand-new guy was killed on a patrol. Nobody could remember his name. He was just the new guy. Driver finally headed to the track, and I followed along through the maze of vehicles. He rearranged a couple of boxes of ammunition sitting on top of the track so I would have room to stretch out. He climbed inside the track where the driver and the squad leader slept. I curled up on the hard metal surface and put my poncho under my head. I fell asleep thinking about the February new guy with no name and his family, sleep rescuing me from the slowly overpowering sadness.

I was awakened during the night by someone who tripped over me. "New guy," Driver yelled to him from his hammock inside the track.

"Doug said for everyone to be here at 1000 tomorrow," the recent arrival responded as he arranged himself on top of the track.

Every time I woke up, I listened for any sounds that would tell me anything. After a night of repeatedly waking, listening, and dropping off, I finally just waited for morning. Eventually, it arrived.

Doug, the squad leader, was an acting sergeant, appeared to be about nineteen years old, and wore his authority easily. In the first few minutes, he was addressed as Robe, Roby, Strobe, and Doug. He nodded to me and then spoke to the assembled squad. "We saddle up at 1430. When we move out from the tracks, it'll be company size. Be at the tracks for inspection at 1400." He looked my way. "Carry a Claymore!"

Everyone started to complain. "Fourteen thirty! That means it's going to be a night mission. That ain't *even* good, Robe."

"Alpha Six don't know what he's doing. If it's company size, he's in charge."

"Whose turn is it to stay back?"

Doug acknowledged the complaints. Then, in order of seniority starting with Doug, they went through the open cases selecting C-rations. They tore open packages, returning items they didn't want to a common box, which everyone went through. I was advised to take anything with fruit, if any was left. None was. Like everyone else, I grabbed three meals.

I spent the rest of the morning cleaning my rifle, loading eighteen rounds into each twenty-round magazine, every fourth or fifth round a tracer. The magazines were stuffed into bandoliers that held seven magazines. After filling two bandoliers, I stopped to calculate. Counting the magazine in my rifle, that would be 270 rounds. With no idea what that meant, I filled more magazines and stuffed them into my pockets. I adjusted and readjusted the web gear and loaded and reloaded the pack, never getting any of it to ride comfortably. Finally admitting to myself there was nothing more to do, I stopped and waited. I had no idea what to expect. Television news had not prepared me.

At 1430, the column of tracks moved out along the dirt road leading northeast from Binh Phuoc, seven or eight soldiers on top of each. I sat near the spot I had slept the night before. Two Six spoke to me over the roar of the engines and clacking of treads along the road. "The object, Carr, is to leave this place the same way you came. Nothing more than that." I nodded and thought to myself I had found the right platoon.

Eventually, the line of tracks left the road and cut single file across a rice paddy. Like a bad carnival ride, the tracks rose and fell as they passed over the dikes, each pass wearing out a little more dike and angering a farmer who rushed out to repair the damaged dike and paddy. Finally, the company's tracks were maneuvered into a circle with the company commander's in the center. In a ritual I didn't understand, the platoon leaders and platoon sergeants walked to the captain's track. Later, the squad leaders were called to join them. The rest of us chose meals from a newly opened box of C-rations and ate to pass the time.

As darkness came, the company moved out, a column eighty men long, winding its way along the ninety-degree turns of the dikes until it moved off the dikes and into calf-deep water. At first, I thought we were crossing a paddy, but there were no dikes visible, and none became visible as we moved. As we trudged across the wash, the water became deeper and the mud at the bottom thicker. Every step was work, and every step became more painful as the mud held the boots in place and lifting one foot out only forced the other deeper. After 100 feet, I was exhausted, and no exit was in sight. With each step, the pain in my lower legs was more intense. Each step took more effort than its predecessor. People passed me, first my own squad and then people I didn't recognize. Again I had worries of being left behind, but here the consequences would be more serious. Doug seemed unbothered by the mud and walked up and down the column encouraging people. He told me to sit for a minute, but the pain returned as soon as I started walking; the effort to extract each leg from the mud felt as though it were ripping the muscles from my shins. Tears started, which I tried to hold back. Each step threatened to be the last.

"People die in war for all sorts of reasons. Some die"—we were told—"because they just give up." I had not understood that when I first heard it. Who would want to die when just a little more effort might save you? Day one in the field, and I thought I understood that it might be true. There was more for me to learn.

The mental struggle joined the physical one. I wasn't going to be able to do this, I told myself. I knew I couldn't do this for a year. I didn't know if I could last the night. If I sat down again, I feared I wouldn't get up. With each step slower than the one before, and each step seeming to pull muscles and tendons from my legs, I struggled on, knowing that eventually I would have to surrender to the pain and quit.

I forced another few steps, and those around me began to slow down. I looked up to notice a wood line had emerged before us. Everyone's pace became more deliberate, and those in front slowly edged out of the wash and onto a wide trail at the edge of the wood line. With too much noise and confusion, the company partially rearranged itself into platoons stretched out over several hundred feet of trail. With the line extending in both directions from me, I feared that moving in either direction to find my squad might only take me farther away from it. Echoed whispers of "Take ten" passed down the line and stopped the movement. Everyone joined those few who had already collapsed along the trail.

We had been walking for less than two hours. The twenty or thirty minutes in the mud had taken everything I had to give. I leaned back on my pack, letting the ground lift it off my shoulders to take as much weight as possible off my back, and suddenly, my shoulders fought with my legs for attention. I felt the indentations the straps had dug into my skin. I fought to keep my eyes open.

Again I flashed back to a training exercise from an earlier night at Fort Lewis. We had been in the field for three or four days, managing three or four hours of sleep a night. That night, we were setting up an ambush along a trail. Lying in the tall grass waiting for our target, I fought to hold off sleep. I began to argue with myself. Finally, the argument that it was only training prevailed. With no idea of how long I had been asleep, I woke up to see the squad I was with moving out. I started to get up to follow them when the wood line exploded with the sound of blanks being fired by M16s. I had almost got up and joined the squad we were to ambush. I fired off a few rounds and then waited. The platoon sergeant came and checked our weapons. Two in the squad had never fired theirs because they too had fallen asleep, awakened only by the sounds of an ambush.

As I sat along another trail reliving that night of a few months earlier, those around me started to get up, and for a moment, I wasn't sure which of the two realities I inhabited. To whispers of "Second Platoon, take point," I moved forward through the line looking for a familiar shadow, but in the dark, I couldn't identify the forms of those I had known for only a day. A hand reached out and grabbed my shoulder from behind. Doug had found me and was following me back to the platoon. "Fall in here," he whispered.

The night walk continued. Now alongside a relatively dry trail, the going was easier. I looked out to the wash and then inward into the nipa palm but could make out nothing. We worked our way down the wood line, following the contours of its river, with only the partial moon's dancing from right shoulder to front to left shoulder providing any indication of the relative direction of our movement. It seemed an aimless walk in the dark.

And suddenly it ended. Platoons began organizing themselves into positions. Soldiers crept away from their units into the dark, setting up Claymores and attaching flares to trip wires. I had been told to keep mine and be quiet until someone told me what to do. I watched just as newly arrived missionaries must watch native ceremonies. Doug found me and took me to the apex of a right angle of soldiers where an M60 machine gun was pointed outward away from the right angle. He told me I had first watch, and he pointed out the hand piece of the radio. "We're ambush patrol two. Every fifteen minutes, battalion will call for a situation report. If everything is okay, just depress the speak button on the handset the number of times they ask you to. If you see something, wake up the two people next to you, let them know there's movement, and then call it in." He gave me his watch. "In one hour exactly, wake the man to the left and give him the watch." He then handed me the Starlight scope, the night-vision device that magnifies existing light thousands of times. "Always look through it with the same eye. You're going to be blind in that eye when you stop looking through it." Then one last time, "You're ambush patrol two."

I crouched behind the machine gun, radio cradled to my ear, and waited for the attack I knew would come on my watch. I handled the night-vision device, the Starlight scope, almost reverently. It came close to making us equals in the night. It was so important that basic training started emphasizing the need to destroy it and the means of doing so to keep it from falling into NVA and eventually into Soviet or Chinese hands. The method that would destroy the scope's inner workings was to fire a tracer down the tube. I did not know if I had a tracer up in my magazine. I resolved always to carry one in my pocket in case I needed to save our technology from the Soviets.

Every few minutes, I looked through the Starlight scope, scanning the green-tinted night it opened to me. As far as I could see, an empty green night spread before me. Every time I thought I saw something move, I got it lined up with a tree in the background. If, after five minutes, the relative positions had not changed, I continued sweeping the night. Static crackled in my ear, and then a voice whispered, "Alpha Papa One, Alpha Papa One. Sitrep up tight, break squelch two times. Over."* It was answered with two bursts of static created by someone depressing the talk button on the radio. This gave us

---

* Sitrep up tight: Situation report good, no activity observed.

a way to provide information when circumstances dictated that we not talk.

The voice in the night continued. "Roger that, Alpha Papa One. Alpha Papa Two, Alpha Papa Two. Sitrep up tight, break squelch one time. Over."

I depressed the receiver once. The voice moved on, confirming that ambush patrol three was all right, and then went silent. I had done nothing but create a burst of static on the company radio net, but I felt I had passed some sort of test. I was somehow now a part of it. At the appointed time, I woke the man on the left. "We're Alpha Papa Two," I whispered as I handed him the watch.

I moved into his spot and took off my helmet. I felt to make sure I knew where my rifle was. I stared out into the blackness until sleep could no longer be held off.

CHAPTER 4

Humpin' the Boonies

The night passed, as would most, without incident. The next day, we split into platoons, and the 2nd Platoon did what it was being paid to do: hump the boonies, walk endlessly through paddies and nipa palm wood lines looking for bad guys. Just three years earlier, Viet Cong battalions moved openly through the rice paddies of Long An Province. Away from the wood lines, the paddies were considered safe during the day. But wood lines were everywhere, and we couldn't walk very far in one direction away from one wood line without approaching another one. In the omnipresent wood lines, I assumed, we would find whatever it was we were looking for.

We humped. Quickly, we were out of sight of the other platoons. Our understrength platoon numbered about twenty-five, and yet I sensed relief on the part of the platoon when it lost visual contact with other elements of the company. We moved slowly along paddy dikes skirting the edge of wood lines that separated one paddy from another. Mud and log bunkers were visible along the edge of the wood lines overlooking the paddies, and someone would be sent to check them out and then blow them up. Virtually every wood line we passed had wood and mud bunkers staring out into the rice paddies, and the muffled explosions of grenades thrown into newly constructed bunkers followed our march.

"It's an endless game," Two Six explained, trying to educate me. "We blow the bunkers every time we come through an area, and as soon as we leave, new ones are constructed."

"Since we can destroy them faster than Charlie rebuilds them, that means we're winning the war," Donald said.

"Yeah, but Charlie makes his out of mud and sticks found at site and can probably make one faster than we can find and destroy it," Two Six said. "Might be that shooting GIs isn't the purpose of the bunkers. Maybe they're here so we'll be here blowing them up. Charlie may just be using a different score-card than we are. Hell, we don't know yet if we're playing the same game."

We walked throughout the morning, Two Six and Doug occasionally stopping to check the map. From the few bits of information available, they were asking how much time it would take to get to the area where we were supposed to set up tonight. The heat grew worse as the hours passed. The occasional stops provided no break from the sun, just an opportunity to sit for a moment and, for those who smoked, to light up. The march continued until noon when we stopped to eat. Lunch provided a few minutes to slip out of our packs.

After twenty minutes, it was more walking, with Doug pacing from the back to front of the squad. He encouraged those who were having trouble. He screamed in whispers at those who broke discipline. He constantly told me to keep my distance, to get closer to or farther from the man in front of me. We walked along a dike that paralleled a wood line twenty meters to our left, thumbs on the selector switch that would take the M16 off safety and to automatic or semi-automatic. We walked past isolated mud-floor houses. Occasionally, a pair of eyes would stare back out of the darkened interiors. We walked past the farmers in conical hats who ignored our passing. The men all looked ancient. They were. The young men were gone, fighting, for whichever side, a war.

As it got hotter, salt stains built up in the fatigues from the sweat that dried as quickly as it dampened a uniform. The pain was different from the night before. Now it was a matter not of muscles feeling like they were being sheared from the bone, but of calling up the strength to fight off the exhaustion. By mid-afternoon, we had been humpin' along paddy dikes for perhaps eight hours, with maybe only five of the entire platoon knowing where we were going or having a chance of getting us there. Like most, I just followed the man in front of me.

We walked on. An hour before sunset we finally stopped in the general area where we would set up our night ambush site and ate.

Again a two-man reconnaissance team set out in the late afternoon with Doug taking the lead. In a little less an hour, they returned and huddled with Two Six. The routine, I was learning that night, was standard across the brigade, one it seemed I was destined to play hundreds of times to make it though the year.

As dusk arrived, the platoon moved to and set up in the pre-night location that had been scouted by the platoon recon team. Then we waited. A half hour to an hour after dark, we pulled up and moved to the permanent ambush site several hundred meters away from pre-night, thereby obscuring the exact location from an enemy that may have been watching us move at dusk. The permanent ambush site was an L formed where two dikes intersected at right angles to each other. One leg of the ambush paralleled a wood line fifty meters away. With a machine gun at the elbow and at each end of the L, we would be able, if necessary, to cover the 360 degrees with machine guns, with two available to aim at the wood line.

Someone tapped me on the shoulder, pointed at the Claymore I was carrying, and then pointed down the dike that ran toward the wood line. I unrolled the cord as I crawled down the dike away from the platoon. I tried to remember everything from training about setting up the device that propels dozens of steel balls packed in front of a pound or so of plastic explosive. Instead, all I could think of was whether anyone except whoever pointed me this way knew I was out here. I didn't want to be simply "The new guy, you remember, the new guy who we accidentally shot on his first mission. What was his name?"

Printed on the Claymore's front are the words "Front Toward Enemy." Of course, the mines were usually set up at night when it was too dark to read. Instead, the convex and concave shapes indicated front and back, the army counting on the nonexistence of a tactile dyslexia. I slid the wires into place, scooped up a little mud to place behind the Claymore, and slowly followed the wires back down the dike. As I approached, I could make out the barrel of an M60 machine gun pointed down the dike at me. I worked around it and connected the Claymore's firing device and laid it by the machine gun. I didn't notice anybody check to see if I'd done everything correctly.

Doug gave out our squad's guard rotations, to start at 1000 hours. Mine was from 0200 to 0300. I was told the man on the M60 side of me would wake me at 0200 and that I would wake the man on the far side of me at 0300. "Oh yeah," I was warned. "Don't fuck with the watch. The time better be right tomorrow morning."

Donald's "You're up" was the next thing I remember. He waited to make sure I was really up, handed me the watch, then slipped into his poncho. "See if you can get a pizza delivered," he whispered as I slid past him.

Another quiet night.

"Highway One's about two klicks* that way," Doug informed a questioner as we set out the next morning. "The ponies will be there at 1000 hours."

The first mission was done. I did nothing wrong. I hadn't earned my way into the squad yet, but I had not knocked myself out of the running

Cold Cokes and beers waited for us at the track. The Puritan in me had chosen the Coke out of fear that there might be a cosmic price to pay for a beer. Crazy? Probably, I told myself, but no less crazy than thinking nobody is keeping score.

---

* Klick: a kilometer, about five-eighths of a mile.

CHAPTER 5

The War Gets Closer

I had completed my first week in the field with the 2nd Platoon, which was yet to make contact—something I knew was not going to continue. Fortunately, it appeared to be approaching slowly.

"Carr! Up!" was what I heard, and in the second or two it took me to process the information, Donnie's elbow was already on its way to my back. Overhead, helicopters circled. Occasional cracks of machine-gun fire could be heard. Rockets and miniguns violated the blackness. Tiny red filaments slashed across the sky while explosions in the woods suppressed the usual night chatter of the birds in the trees.

Donald, who had made sure those next to him were awake, then crawled into the position where he had been manning the radio since taken over by Two Six when things started to happen. "First Platoon's been hit. They're maybe a klick and a half from us. A point element headed more or less our way walked right up on them. One Six wiped out the point element, but then they started taking fire from whoever they were point for—most likely a platoon. Point element could have been local VC guiding their brothers to somewhere a day or two's march from here. Some Higher says the bad-guy platoon might be headed our way now. Not *even* very likely. They're into the wood line and disappeared. They are not going to try anything with gunships on station."

Donald was right. We saw nothing the rest of that night.

The next morning, we humped down to check on the 1st Platoon. They were sitting around as we stopped at their position, not acknowledging the two Vietnamese bodies thirty feet up from them, collapsed across a dike. Two Six stopped to talk to One Six. I strained to listen.

"I don't know if someone saw us setting up or maybe even picked us up moving to pre-night. They didn't just stumble across us. Their point knew we were close. One had a grenade in his hand when I shot him. They got to within thirty or forty feet. Our machine gunner froze. I got one with my .45, and then the machine gun opened up. Then we started getting fire from a few hundred meters away. Nothing accurate. Nobody hurt. We were lucky, though. If the point element had waited for more of its unit to get there, we'd have been in a world of hurt."

I thought about Donnie's comment last night and those from One Six this morning. I asked anyone if my puzzlement made sense. "If it was a point element and something happened with the machine gun and you're going to attack, why hadn't he pulled his pin? Maybe they weren't looking for the 1st Platoon. If you look at the general direction they're headed, then if the 1st is somewhere else, they end up where we were last night. Maybe Higher was right, and they were heading for us."

Donnie stared a minute, then asked, "Why, do you really think that they might have been after us?"

"Could have been. A point element is not there to engage. It finds us, and either finds a way of going around us or bringing the force it has with it to bear. But it doesn't attack us with two men."

"And it matters *because*?"

"Maybe they saw us moving, not the 1st Platoon, and that means maybe we did something wrong. Maybe we were the hunted. That would explain why the point didn't wait for the rest of their platoon. They hadn't yet found us. They were headed where they believed we were, didn't expect the 1st Platoon to be where it was. If the 1st Platoon hadn't set up where it had, they would have reached us 1,000 meters later, right through there. Maybe they did just stumble into the 1st Platoon."

"Or maybe," said Donnie "it was local VC guiding its NVA guests somewhere. Maybe to some ARVN base. Could have been a lot of things. Could have found a better way of carrying a hand grenade. All the 'what ifs' and 'could haves' aren't good for the digestion. Keep speculating without evidence, and they're going to transfer you to Intelligence."

I thought I should be learning from Donnie rather than arguing with him. But I had some hard questions, too. Why would a point element attack something that had to be a lot larger than itself?

Two Six shouted, "Saddle up," and all speculation stopped. Everyone took one last look at the bodies as we moved out. I tried not to think about the dead, but couldn't help wondering about their stories. I wanted to feel the right way about them, but I didn't know what that was.

The next day and night proved uneventful. The following morning, the ponies arrived to return us to Binh Phuoc.

It was becoming clear that we knew very little about the enemy, little about either his priorities or his tactics. Surely, in a war lasting this long, we should have found out more than it appeared we had. Last night, an enemy point element either attacked or stumbled upon and fought an American unit it knew was larger. Why? We had no idea.

CHAPTER 6

Light Shows

In my first two weeks with the platoon, nobody had shot at us. We had been in the field when units around us were hit. We had watched as red and green tracers several klicks away arced gracefully toward each other through the darkness. They had yet to arc through that darkness to or away from me. The monsoon that would fill the paddies was near. The weather, I hoped, would be the only thing that changed as the platoon explored this mission's area of operation.

Maybe the army was holding the fighting off because if I didn't fight, they would not have to pay me. When I reported to the company pay officer for my first pay envelope, I was told they did not have an envelope for me. I was told to go to battalion headquarters, which I did. At battalion headquarters, they told me to catch a ride to brigade finance headquarters in Tan An. They could probably tell me. Nobody offered to call or look up anything for me, so I caught a truck going to Tan An. I explained my problem to the MPs at the gate at Tan An and was sent to Finance, where I learned my pay envelope was sent to Bravo Company back at Binh Phuoc. I could go pick it up there. I got back to Binh Phuoc, made my way to Bravo Company, and found their pay officer at the other end of a long line. I got in line, progressed to the front, and then got yelled at by the pay officer for not requesting pay properly. I said I wasn't requesting pay; I said that I had been sent all over the brigade trying to find mine, and I was told it was probably here. He went through his list. He found me. So, in finest getting-paid style, I came to attention, held a salute until he returned it, and belted out, "PFC Carr reports for pay, sir!"

I had used one whole day on something that could have been handled at battalion with one phone call. I told myself that if I ever got a job in the rear, I would certainly take care of any problems within my reach. One whole day off was lost for me, I complained. Doug interrupted my tirade.

"Was anyone shooting at you today?" asked Doug.

"No, but—"

Doug interrupted, "Then it was good duty. Just as much time used if you had been doing something else. Nobody shooting at you."

Robe the Strobe sometimes seemed the only one who understood the way to fight this war.

Today's walk in the sun proved uneventful so far. We had waded across a canal rather than chance a small suspicious looking bridge. The ten minutes it took for fatigues to dry out gave us a temporary break from the omnipresent heat.

Half an hour before sunset, we stopped 100 meters from what appeared to be the remains of a bombed Buddhist temple. A recon team quickly looked at a map with Two Six and then set out to find our pre-night and night locations. Two Six had the rest of us clean our weapons to get out any moisture we might have picked up crossing the canal and then fire a couple of tracer rounds at the temple to make sure our rifles worked. He stepped up first. Someone called, "Door," and Two Six put three tracers into the door. Several more stepped up, and tracer after tracer found its way into the doors of the temple ruins. I was impressed at how good they were. I fired a single round from a sitting position and watched it sink into the bottom of the door.

"Wow, got him right square in the ankle," a voice behind me said.

"Lethal ankle shot," I said, and then satisfied my rifle worked, I watched the others fire.

I wanted to say something about how good they were but couldn't come up with a way that wouldn't be clumsy. Instead, I told them that if we were ever attacked by a temple, they're the guys I'd want with me. Donald jumped in describing a

top-secret briefing he had overheard about temples turning
into Viet Cong companies.

Two Six quickly shut our talking down with a serious "Get
ready" and then talked to the recently returned recon team as
they studied a map. "Everyone in the area knows where we are
now. Take us to pre-night, Alabama," he directed the leader of
the point squad.

For the first time, it dawned on me that every two-man
recon team that was sent out to find the ambush locations had
a squad leader on it as well as someone senior from another
squad whom the squad leader selected. And also for the first
time, I had to acknowledge the thrill that the prospect of that
job gave me. I tried to imagine myself in the position of selecting an ambush site. What did you look for? What did you try to
avoid? The brief expenditure of imagination yielded to the cog-
nitive needs of moving out.

A quick serpentine walk placed us 600 meters from the
afternoon's hootch. Empty-handed troops crawled out along
the dikes as if they were setting up flares and Claymores. We
waited for night. When it came, our silhouettes, held prisoner
by twilight against the horizon, were freed, and we moved
again. Half an hour and 300 meters in the dark took us in and
out of pre-night to our permanent night location. This time,
the trip flares and Claymores were actually set up. Doug got
out his record of who had done what, including what time
people had last been on guard. He rotated us one place forward in time and gave each of us our watch hours.

I was scheduled for a midnight shift and fell asleep as soon
as given the OK. I didn't sleep long. Green tracers announced
someone's presence as they raced overhead close enough for
their whistling to be heard. Because the water was beginning
to fill the paddies, we had been sleeping on the dikes rather
than behind them. Around me, people were rolling off the
dike into two or three inches of water.

"Make sure everyone knows to hold their fire," Two Six
whispered. Quietly, the order went down the line.

I looked up and could no longer see tracers, but still could hear the distinct chug of a Chinese-made machine gun. Soon the fire again became accurate, rounds whistling overhead or impacting into the dike in front of us. Then the fire moved on down the dike in the direction of our pre-night. I had to admit that those nights when other units were in contact and tracers raced through the darkness it was all eerily beautiful—lines of green or red drawn across the blackness. I felt guilty for even thinking about the aesthetics of a firefight. Tonight, it was someone else's turn to watch. I would be unable to establish the aesthetic distance to see anything except danger.

I was a reluctant soldier. I had not volunteered for the war. But for the first time, I was forced to restrain a desire to fight back. Someone was shooting at me, and for the first time, my attitude toward the war was not political or a rationalization of a basic desire to stay alive. Someone I had been perfectly willing to leave alone wanted to kill me, and if they were going to shoot at me, I wanted to shoot back. I ran a cleaning patch down the barrel of my rifle in case any moisture had condensed there, and I waited either for the opportunity to shoot back or for the feeling to pass.

Again the "Don't shoot back" order was passed down the line. Someone explained to those close enough to hear him, "If they're willing to show us the location of their machine gun, there's a lot more in the wood line than just one guy with a machine gun. They know we've moved into the neighborhood. They'd just like our mailing address."

A few minutes later, Two Six was back in contact with the helicopter gunship headed our way. "Estimate Chi Com machine gun one-two-five meters at sixty degrees from my location. Will advise as soon as I hear you arriving."

More rounds whistled past, some ricocheting off the paddies in front of us. Some could be heard impacting into the dike. Thoughts that they had found us rose and then vanished as the light show moved on through our position and again headed down the dike.

"That's a lot of ammo for Charlie to use," Two Six specu-lated. "Either they want us pretty bad or they've got a better supply system than we've been told."

Those whose watches had coincided with the firing kept searching the area to our front with Starlight scopes, making sure that bullets were the only thing probing for our location. The rest of us waited, beginning to feel the chill from lying in the few inches of water, which was now working its way up our uniforms.

Two Six was back on the radio as the sound of a helicopter in the distance joined the other sounds of night. The sound of the machine gun stopped. Two Six broke open an M79 grenade launcher, basically a sawed-off shotgun that fires a sin-gle 40-millimeter grenade. Then, pointing the barrel upward, he inserted a strobe light in the barrel. The strobe light was vis-ible to those above us, but not to those on the ground. In a matter of seconds, the helicopter found us, circled, and headed down the sixty-degree compass reading that it had been given earlier. Its rockets tore into the wood line near the area from which we had been taking fire. I could not help thinking how much they looked like the special-effect photon torpedoes from *Star Trek*, like a ball of light accelerating down-ward. The next pass brought the thousands-of-rounds-per minute fire of the gunship's miniguns. At that rate of fire, the tracers appeared as an unbroken red ribbon between sky and ground. After several more passes through the area, the heli-copter went off station. We received no fire from the machine gun or from anywhere else in the wood line.

This was, on a small scale, the way those at the top— "Higher than Higher"—had chosen to fight the war. Lure the enemy into a fight by sending out a few tempting morsels and, when he went after them, bring in the firepower. It made a lot less sense if you were one of the tempting morsels. This time it appeared to work out all right, but I didn't have time to pon-der my role as bait in the great scheme of things.

I was next up on watch, so I moved down to the intersection of two dikes where our machine gun and Starlight scope were.

I scanned the green-lit distance in front of us, moving the scope slowly to the wood line, then up and down the length of it. For the first time, I noticed the wood line in front of us wasn't unbroken. There was a large gap of open paddy 100 meters or so to the left. As I explored the opening, I thought I detected motion. I searched and found the cause. I whispered, "Damn," as I looked again. Everyone asked, "What's up?"

"Man running across the open area to the left. Really moving," I reported. "Came out of the area we were taking fire from. Doesn't appear to be carrying a weapon."

My voice must have sounded a bit excited as Doug's "Just be cool and stay with him" seemed design to calm whatever urgency I had induced. The runner crossed the break and disappeared into the wood line.

Two Six asked for a report.

"Just one guy. Was running out of the wood line in front of us to the one down the line on the left. Didn't appear to be carrying a weapon. He looked heavy, not thin like most of them, but damn, could he move."

"Was probably the legendary Vietnamese runner Hop Along Fat Tan," Donald whispered to me. "Did he have one or two legs?"

Doug's "At ease" helped suppress any laughter.

I had finally seen a live member of the other side. Others seemed more impressed with the fact than I thought they should be. Several had been in half a dozen or more firefights and had seen nothing more than the muzzle flashes that told you where fire was coming from. I didn't have time to think about the significance of my first sighting of one of the bad guys. Overhead, the sound of shells popping broke the silence, and illumination flares parachuting downward lit up the area around us.

"Call in and find out what's going on, Carr!" Two Six yelled from the middle of the line where he had gone checking up on everyone.

"Alpha Six, Alpha Six. Alpha Two Six Oscar. Over."

"Two Six, this is Alpha Six. Go ahead. Over."

Before I could respond, Two Six worked his way down the line and took the handset. "Alpha Six Oscar, this is Two Six Actual. Kill the illumination. We didn't ask for it. We're in the middle of a paddy, and you're lighting us up for the bad guys to pick off. Over."

More illumination rounds discharged their canisters overhead and parachuted down. And more. Fifteen minutes after the first request to stop, the paddy was still illuminated against the night sky. The moving shadows they created had us seeing glimpses of Vietnamese who were not there.

Down the line, someone yelled that he had seen someone move into the hootch situated perhaps 150 meters behind us. The soldier stuck with his story even though others who had been looking that direction insisted it was shadows from the illumination.

If he was right, we might have bad guys to the front and rear—if any were left out front. Another illumination round popped.

Someone yelled, "Movement!" and opened up in the direction of the house. The whole platoon then opened up on the house for a minute or two. Our position was now exposed. But apparently, the wood line and the house were clear since no one was firing back. The rest of the night passed with quiet situation reports.

We checked out the house the next morning. Like many in the area, it had a bunker built inside. Apparently, the family had spent the night there. Nobody was hurt. The mama-san yelled at us, pointing out damage done by our bullets. By morning, the wood line revealed many bunkers that were left to another platoon to blow. Around the area from which we had taken machine-gun fire, only a few spent shell casings could be found. They had vanished and taken with them almost any indication of their presence.

The memory of this evening's light show would soon fade for most of the platoon. All that most had was a memory of the light show, soon to be collapsed into memories of a dozen other light shows. I had the image of someone running through a green-lit landscape to help preserve this one.

In a year, if I survived, there would almost certainly be only one person who would remember a heavy Vietnamese running between two wood lines through that Delta night, who would have that bit of the world for his story. Our stories are a complex weave. Some of the threads necessary to understanding us belong not to us, but to others. We all remember incidents with other people, incidents that are long off their radar. There are words and acts of ours which only they remember, which we have long ago forgotten. Still, most of our individual stories are like the memories of a heavy soldier running through the night and a discussion of it which, almost certainly, only I will remember. So much of our own collective story is known by only one other person and will someday vanish with him, its pieces not even left on the cutting room floor.

CHAPTER 7

Folk Tales

War brings in train its own folk tales and urban legends, and Vietnam was no exception. Some of the stories may have been based on something that was at one time true. Some may even be true, but a positive relation to truth has nothing to do with whether or not they survive and are passed on to become part of some group's lore. The interesting part of the equation here is why those who were skeptics about almost everything they heard here not only found some of them particularly worth passing on, but also clearly regarded them as true.

One was the tale of black syphilis. If you hadn't been warned of it by the time you got to your unit, you would hear about it very soon after arriving. Black syphilis was, the story went, an incurable and easy-to-transmit form of syphilis. The military was not going to allow soldiers to take it home to spread across the country, in part because taking it home to wives and lovers would not be nice, but also because knowledge of its source and a widespread infection rate might weaken support for the war. So be careful was the warning. Should you be diagnosed with it, first, your family would be notified that you were missing in action. Second, you would be shipped to a colony in the Philippines to be held under armed guard where you would await the development of a cure. The flaws and difficulties with the story were obvious, but that did not matter. In the insanity of war, it made sense.

The other was also a tale of sex and prostitution. Working with the Viet Cong were prostitutes who would insert a razor blade into themselves. Usually, the story ended there as soldiers hearing it cringed and waved off the need to finish the story.

It was, after all, an army of twenty-year-olds. What topic would most likely survive? What urban legend would you think more likely to get the attention of a twenty-year-old who listens to rock and roll and be certain to get passed on to the next generation? Pretty clearly, it is not going to be the World War II story of someone who mailed a rifle or a jeep home one piece at a time.

Some of war's legends endure because they are true. There is behavior so strange that the stories must be true. Maybe the anthropologist or folklorist can explain why some stories survive to be passed on; it may be a property quite unrelated to their truth. The true ones are at a disadvantage: you cannot modify them without somebody knowing that is not what happened. For example, here's one I saw in Oakland on my way to Vietnam. It seems like it should have become a military legend, but I never heard a reference to it or anything like it. We were sleeping in massive several-hundred-bed barracks waiting for our name to be called. One baby-faced eighteen-year-old was constantly giggling or laughing or running from bunk to bunk. Finally, with the attention of three or four of us, he got a suitcase out from under his bed. He nodded, indicating he wanted us to get closer. None of us would, so he opened it. It was full of fireworks. He laughed uncontrollably. How could he have gotten this far? Even if he was fishing for a discharge on grounds of psychological problems incompatible with the best interests of the United States Army, he should have been given an Oscar and helped with his packing.

I had heard dozens of such stories in my first month in Vietnam, like those of Viet Cong attacking bases where the bodies found stacked in front of food storage carried not weapons but can openers and crude hand-drawn maps of the kitchens, or those involving soldiers with almost superhero-like abilities to stay inside a base camp for several days without being noticed. Very soon in that second month, the new guys would ask about the camp in the Philippines or about the devices that hold razor blades in place. All of the others had failed to make the cut, even the ones I knew to be true—the boy going to war with the bag of fireworks. I did not know the beginning or ending of that story. But I knew, almost certainly, that each part only added to the story its measure of sadness.

CHAPTER 8

Coasting and Vampires

The usual twenty-hour standdowns between missions at Binh Phuoc had their routines and rhythms. We got back. We cleaned our gear, and not having any place to call home, we left it on the tracks. We searched for a company shower that still had water in it, occasionally threatening to shoot the members of the rear echelon, the REMFs, who tried to order us out of their company showers. With some justification, they believed we were just that crazy. If we had time, we went to Tan An, brigade headquarters, to stock up on beer and Coke and to visit their PX. During the day, between hot meals in the mess hall, most of the platoon went to the enlisted men's club, secured one of the tables stuffed into its 500 square feet—adequate space since there was rarely more than one line company in the camp at a time—and wrote letters. Others just vanished, not to reappear until we prepared to move out the next day. I fell in with the letter writers.

The letters home created an unanticipated moral dilemma for me. Seen through the distorting fog of war, it went something like this: should I tell everyone back home it isn't so bad over here so they would worry less, or should I be as honest as my limited perception would let me be and cause worry? The downside to the former, revealed through the haze, was that my family might not be adequately prepared for something happening to me. The upside to brutal honesty was that maybe they'd be more ready for it and be able to accept it when the bad news came. It seemed the most real and most intransigent question I could face. Do I play the danger down or up? After a June mission when four soldiers in the company were killed, I resolved the dilemma as follows: my letter home said three were killed. I thought I was letting them know it was bad, but hiding a bit just how bad. At that time, in that place, it really seemed to make sense.

Letters and food and talk filled the brief time we had back in the base camp. Slowly, the members of the squad opened up to me. I saw that I was being accepted. In the worst of circumstances, a friend turned out to be the best thing to have.

Too soon into a standdown, it was time to move out. Less than twenty-four hours was deemed necessary to let our feet dry out enough to stave off jungle rot. Less than twenty-four hours is what we got.

This time, the column of tracks followed a different road, this one leading northwest out of Binh Phuoc. We passed through villages where young kids held up three fingers representing the three lines of the South Vietnamese flag. The gesture served many purposes. It was intended to say we're on your side, so don't shoot. But mostly, it was part of the constant appeal in villages and cities for anything we might give them— food, candy, cigarettes. Some made a sadistic game of it, treating the kids like ducks in a shooting gallery. They would throw cans of C-rations at, not to, the children in the towns we drove through. I was too new to feel or understand the hatred they felt for the Vietnamese in the towns. I stared blankly at those on the track behind me. I wanted to believe we were the good guys, but some people made it very hard.

Doug had been staring at me, perhaps reading the play of emotions on my face. "Some people have been here one battle too long, one KIA squad member too long. Don't waste the energy that you're going to need to finish that sixth month and seventh month where you can't win."

Eventually, the column left the road and headed across the paddies to some preordained spot. The paddies had not yet begun to collect water from the coming monsoons, and the farmers were spending time repairing and strengthening dikes that would have to hold the water that the rains would bring. For now, the paddies were empty, and rather than tearing up a rice crop, the tons of weight suspended on the two tracks at the point where the armored personnel carriers crossed the dikes wore down the dikes. The Vietnamese followed us through their fields redoing their earlier dike repair. The damage and repair cycle continued until, like wagon trains in the last century, we chose a spot and circled up.

The three platoons moved out independently. Looking back at the circle of APCs with their machines guns pointed out at the paddy and their mortars set up in the center and then noting the twenty-five of us in our understrength platoon made me feel particularly vulnerable. On my first mission, we had moved out as a company. This time, three platoons headed in different directions. As we had prepared to move out, everyone else in the squad seemed up, ready for the mission.

Snaking along the dikes through the midday sun, we were quickly out of sight of the tracks and the other platoons. Located for the moment in the middle of large open paddies, we moved quickly. As we were forced closer to wood lines by the terrain, the pace slowed. At times, we passed by the doorways of the mud and thatch hootches. Children stood in doorways as we passed, not begging like the children in the towns. They just stared. And always the heat. Nowhere a moment's shade.

I had failed to notice any change, but the squad leaders and Two Six were huddled as the rest of the platoon crouched down, staring into the wood line we had been paralleling. Two from another squad were called forward and joined Two Six and the Strobe. I finally broke down and gave Donald a "What's up?" look.

"Fresh bunkers," he whispered. "No way to get to them from the side. Someone's going to have to cross a lot of open ground."

I shrugged to indicate I saw nothing, and then Donnie extended his left arm. I sighted along his extended arm and could see the bunker at the edge of the wood line, its gun port facing into the paddy. It appeared to be about two feet high and three-by-three on the sides. Set back against the wood line, it would provide an occupant a view of all the paddy in front of it from the gun port.

"Keep going right," said Donald after I found it, continuing to move his arm slowly in that direction. "The grass they pulled out and put on the corners of the bunker to hide its outline is the same color as the brush growing around there. It's been tended to lately. Maybe today."

I never would have thought of looking for color differences. There was just too much to learn.

Twenty meters to the right was a second. Beyond that, a third. As I stared at the bunkers, one of the two who had been called forward worked his way across open paddy keeping thirty or forty meters to the left of the leftmost bunker. Exposed like that, he had no chance if anyone was in the wood line in front of him. In that moment, no syllogism about everyone being mortal was needed to understand that war was really deadly and that I was at war. I saw myself walking into a wood line with the platoon fifty meters behind me, staring intently for any sign of anything unusual. But what would it matter if I did see something? I couldn't then turn around and walk back.

The real drama being played out before me brought me out of my imaginary one. The soldier reached the edge of the wood line twenty or so meters to the left of the first bunker. He could now approach it from the side without being vulnerable to anyone in the bunker. "Approaches will be booby-trapped"— I remembered the lectures from training and understood his deliberateness as he approached the bunker. Removing a grenade from his web gear, he tossed it into the back of the bunker and sprinted back the ten meters he had just so cautiously crossed. The bunker disintegrated. A few minutes later, the second joined it. Then the third. Each would be rebuilt as soon as we were out of the area. Two Six's radio telephone operator called in the destroyed bunkers. We marched on.

Just past mid-afternoon, Two Six stopped the march as we approached a small family dwelling. Two Six had the squad leaders from the other squads set up around the hooch. The 2nd Squad entered the hooch with him. Inside, a woman and two children watched as we sat on the dirt floor in front of a cooking fire. She sent the oldest of the children out into the paddy, and the child returned in a few minutes with an old man who was speaking excitedly. We understood him, if not his words. He was both afraid of us and offended by us.

Two Six tried to calm him with his voice. "Papa-san, we just want a few minutes out of the sun." He then offered the man a cigarette. The man took it and squatted among us. He occasionally said something none of us understood. We replied with phrases he didn't understand, but in a quiet, nonthreatening tone. He finished the cigarette. Instead of offering him another, Doug handed him an unopened pack from the C-rations. The man took the pack, but didn't open it. He placed it in a small basket on the floor by the fire. He then took a pot from the fire and offered us tea.

None of us spoke Vietnamese, and we were pretty sure he didn't speak English. I took it on myself to do some impromptu translations of his comments. I waited for the next thing the Vietnamese said. "Two Six, he wants to know just where we Yankee dogs will set up our ambush tonight?"

"Ask if he knows Ho Chi Minh personally," suggested Two Six.

"Hoa mau, choi hoi" sounded to me as if it should be Vietnamese.

The man mumbled something to his wife, no doubt about the crazy Americans.

Again, I stepped into my role as mock interpreter. "Says he'll bet any of us five piasters the Reds will win the World Series."

Others inside the hootch started giving me questions to ask when the radio interrupted the afternoon tea as well as my routine. Two Six's radio telephone operator moved the radio to Two Six. "This is Alpha Six. Higher wants a sitrep from Alpha Six. Needs to know where we are, what we're up to right now."

"Alpha Six, this is Two Six. Over."

A pause as Two Six listened to the company commander's inquiries.

"Roger that, Alpha Six. No bunkers since our last sitrep. Setting up right now to send the recon team out. Roger that.

Out." He took a final sip of tea. "Mount up," he muttered. "Alpha or Higher says we could have humped ten more minutes before sending out our recon team.

I felt as though a piece of one puzzle had slipped into place. Why was the platoon relieved to give up the rest of the company's firepower and go out on its own? Perhaps, under nobody's watchful eye, we could occasionally take a few minutes off from the war.

Eventually, I was sent outside with several others, replacing those who had kept watch on the surrounding nipa palm while the rest of the platoon sat either in the peasant's hooch or in its shade. I had been called to rejoin those who were in the war, keeping an eye on the ominous wood lines that surrounded us. Ten meters down the dike, one of the veterans from another squad stared intently at the wood line. His demeanor reminded me that the war wasn't gone, just in recess. I must have still looked puzzled and not totally comprehending.

"Hey, new guy," he yelled, waiting for me to turn toward him. "We got here fifteen, maybe twenty, minutes early. Fifteen or twenty before we needed to send out the recon team. If the Oscars only have to fight for half a war, no point in us fighting a whole one. Just wouldn't feel right. Gotta get the recon team and our location and sunset back in balance. Coasting? No, we just arrived fifteen mikes early. Won't happen often. Enjoy it when it does. Think of it this way. Every thirty missions where we stop fifteen minutes early add up to one whole day less in the field."

I would have liked some answers. Could we really get away with this? Did other units ever do this? I knew better than to ask. Five minutes later, the recon team reappeared, and we formed up by squad. Somewhere right now, others had to have called "King's X" for part of the afternoon. But a counter-thought rose to challenge every thought. Somewhere right now, someone who couldn't or wouldn't coast is dying. His mother doesn't know yet. I didn't know how to feel.

We came in the next morning. Once again, we weren't to know why. Late in the afternoon, I walked into the enlisted men's club but found nobody from the squad there. Several from another squad were talking about someone who had "gone vampire." It was a phrase I had not yet heard. I opened the can of potato chips I had just purchased from the base PX and handed them to one of the squad members as a way of buying my way into another squad's conversation. He passed them around. I slipped quietly into a seat at the end of the table.

"Yeah, he's really short. Maybe three or four days left in country. So short that when he laces up his boots, you can only see the top of his head."

"I heard he's from Charlie Company. A lot of their short-timers go vampire. It's because their CO's a jerk. You don't *even* want to be around him."

"That ain't *even* it, man. Everybody's CO is a jerk. That's how they got to be CO. Going vampire's the smart thing."

I had learned what a short-timer was, someone whose year-long tour in country was about over, whose time left in country was short. Hence the "short" jokes—so short that you can load him in a magazine or so short he's got to look up to see a dog's belly. Coming up with new ways of describing how short you were could sustain an otherwise dying conversation for another ten minutes. What I hadn't heard before or managed to figure out was the vampire imagery. I sat quietly, grabbed some of the potato chips that had made their way around the table to me, and waited for someone to say enough to let me figure it out. They upped the ante.

"I'm going to see him," one volunteered. "Anybody else want to?"

"Sure," I said—my first words since joining their table. A third got up and followed as we made our way out, and we set out in the direction of Charlie Company's bunkers. Some of the bunkers were two stories, with a .50-caliber machine gun up top and an M60, roughly .30 caliber, down below. Those pulling guard duty at night worked alternating shifts, with those awake upstairs on the .50 and the lower-level serving as sleeping quarters for the two hours its occupants would be off.

Our guide peered into the first we encountered, found nothing, and kept walking.

"Why do you call them vampires?" I asked, hoping to glean some inkling of what I was looking for.

"Some guys who've been on the line for close to their year begin to panic that they've survived this long only to get killed right before they DEROS. It's happened. So as soon as they've been told they're out of the field, they move into one of the bunkers. They sleep in the day when it's safer to sleep. They leave only to go to the latrine. They live on C-rations. Dark, when Charlie's out, they stay awake. Sleep all day in a bunker. Awake at night in the bunker. Always in the dark. Vampires."

Several bunkers later, we still hadn't found anyone. Somehow, in the logic of that moment, that we didn't find him confirmed his existence for the other two. "We must be late," claimed the guide. Lucky bastard's already gone home." The other nodded in agreement. By the time I found the squad for dinner, they had already heard about how some guy from the 1st Squad had talked to a guy from Charlie Company who had lived for three days in a bunker. They stared and asked, "Well, is there a Binh Phuoc vampire?"

I started to sit down, and although they were sensing a lecture coming that they could not gracefully avoid, I started, "If you had three days left here and there were occasional shots fired this way, wouldn't you think it reasonable to go vampire, and live in the bunker for two days, and then in daylight hitch a ride to the airfield? Might you be tempted to spend two days protected?"

They nodded, and I continued. "So you admit two days make sense. Then isn't it reasonable to make sure you get to that last four days? So you spend four days in a bunker. Same, same, no? Seems to me you ought to get in that bunker the day you arrive and stay until it's your day to go home."

"Well?" one asked.

"Well what?

"Is there a vampire in Charlie or not?"

"Nah," I answered. "Went home yesterday. Just missed him. I gotta go get one of the bunkers registered in my name. I'm already two months late in signing up for my bunker. Since you'll be home, could you arrange to have someone wake me in May?"

CHAPTER 9

Malaria Monday

Days in the field were spent walking—walking through rice paddies beginning to fill with water, along trails at the edges of wood lines, in the wet, clay-like mud where the nipa palm jungles grew. When we stopped, our eyes would search the distance, but for people doing something as serious as we were doing, the concerns voiced in our conversation were anything but.

What mattered when we stopped was what C-rations everyone had or even what day of the week it was. C-ration meals came twelve different boxes to a case, each box containing a main course and a dessert. The box also had a utility package with instant coffee, a pack of four cigarettes, a plastic spoon, and a few sheets of toilet paper. When you were fighting to stay awake, half an instant coffee packet and a mouthful of water was good for an hour or two.

Of the twelve main courses, about six of them could be eaten without too much complaining. The most generally pronounced edible main courses were the beans and frankfurters, spaghetti with beef chunks, something called "turkey" (which didn't taste bad, just not at all like turkey), beef and potatoes, and, for some, the boneless chicken. The second can held the dessert. The most-sought after was fruit, a pear or a peach in syrup. Usually, you found yourself stuck with pound cake, or the pecan roll, or what was believed to be a cookie. The one absolutely inedible meal was ham and lima beans. Anyone who got that just accepted the fact he was going to go without one meal this mission. To save space in our packs, we would stuff the ration cans into a sock that could carry three or four meals and attach the sock to our packs. In the field, we ate the meals out of the can without heating them. If we were on the tracks, we would heat them by burning C-4 plastic explosive. Hot or cold, three meals provided 3,600 high-fat, low-fiber calories. A good day was one where you got fruit.

A recurring topic of conversation when we stopped for a ten- or fifteen-minute break was what day of the week it was. In the field, we had two markers for the day of the week. If we were with the tracks on Sunday morning, Two Six would always find some way to delay departure until after "Spanish Hour," sixty minutes of Latin music every Sunday morning on Armed Forces Radio.

The other time marker was the malaria pill. Monday was the day that Doc—all platoon medics were called that—would pass out malaria pills. The pill we got was large and orange, and a common side effect was diarrhea. Every Monday, we would get a call reminding the medic that today was Monday and it was time to have everyone take the pill. Doc passed out the pills and made sure we at least put it our mouth. For some, getting malaria seemed like a reasonable price to pay to get off the line, and malaria tablets became part of the ecosystem. There was more to the pill than what it was protecting us from or how it might be avoided. What it really meant was that for a brief period of time, we knew what day it was.

As long as it wasn't Monday, the day of the week made no difference in any way to our lives. But once or twice a week, as we sat eating or getting our packs off our backs for a few minutes, someone would ask the question, as someone just had today, and until it was time to get up and start moving again, nothing would matter more.

We had stopped for a ten-minute break when someone asked the question, "Doc, isn't it getting close to pill day?"

"Why? You think you're going to get pregnant if I don't give them to you on time?"

"Friday," someone said. "Today's Friday."

"Not *even*, man. We took Doc's orange pill yesterday. Gotta be Tuesday. Isn't that right Doc?"

"That wasn't *even* yesterday," another said. "Day before yesterday, maybe."

"Closer to a week. It's Saturday or Sunday."

There was a girl in college I had first met and asked out for coffee on a Wednesday. I knew having an ulterior motive violated the truthseeking spirit of the discussion, but I always defended Wednesday. Anyway, I didn't know it wasn't Wednesday. "I was thinking maybe it's Wednesday," I said.

"Man, you always think it's Wednesday. You got somewhere you gotta be on Wednesday?"

Eventually, the radio telephone operator called in to battalion with our situation report and asked what day it was. Because he had not taken up the cause of one day himself, most would believe him. Only Two Six's "Saddle up and move out" ended our half-hour lunch break and discussion. Ten to twenty minutes into the march, a loud-enough-to-be-heard whisper would try to be the last word: "It's Thursday, you bozos." In unison, half a dozen other days were muttered in reply.

At the base camp at Binh Phuoc, there was a sign by the chapel announcing the day. Nobody bothered to check. Nobody ever looked. There, in the camp, it just did not seem to matter. Why would it?

Later that morning, we got the call, and Doc passed out malaria pills.

CHAPTER 10

Hearts and Minds

Some sufficiently removed from battle spoke of the war as a struggle for the hearts and minds of the Vietnamese people. The constant emphasis on body counts suggested hearts and minds were not what we were after. The smoking gun was the simple fact that if you seek converts, you don't give automatic weapons to a bunch of twenty-year-old missionaries and send them out in the charge of twenty-three-year-olds. If the battle was for the hearts and minds of the Vietnamese, then the summer of 1969 was not a good time of year in Long An Province.

The pattern of missions continued for most of June with a few exceptions—two or three days of walking through rice paddies and nipa palm during the day and setting up ambushes at night, followed by a night in the base camp. Contacts were very few, and it seemed mostly matters of their choice. And we usually did all right if we moved as a platoon or, as we were doing more and more, as a squad, but when we traveled as a company, somehow we always found a way to lose the hearts-and-minds battle.

The rain came more often as the month wore on, starting to fill rice paddies with the water necessary for the rice. Now armored personnel carriers were destroying not only dikes when the tracks were off the road, but also newly planted rice. We tried to minimize the damage, with each APC following as closely as possible to the track marks in front of it. But every mission, we watched some farmer observe the destruction of what he had just planted.

The procedure was for the farmer to make a claim against the government for the damage we had done, and the

American serving as district adviser would see that he was compensated. Of course, a percentage of the payment for damages was skimmed off by local Vietnamese officials. But even paying generously for damages missed the point.

The point was there in the faces of the farmers who would try unsuccessfully to wave us off as we approached their newly planted rice. The rice was more to them than the money they would sell it for. It was a connection with the land and with ancestors. It was the activity that bound them to neighbors.

During the day, newly planted rice was destroyed by the tons of the tracked metal boxes plowing through them. At night, Viet Cong tax collectors would lay claim to their per-centage of what was left.

But even when the tracks were circled and just sitting there, the contingencies of fighting in a populated area pro-vided other ways to alienate the hearts and minds that were left. Just off a road, at the upswing of the Delta monsoon, the company found a night location, which, while muddy, at least didn't have us sleeping in water. Perhaps 100 meters away was a farmer's hootch with two stacks of something (grain? hay? thatch?) I couldn't identify in the half light a few feet from the house. Its effect was to offer a sheltered approach to within 150 meters from us. It was the logical way for someone to try to approach us without being seen. Two volunteered to go set up flares attached to trip wires along the approach. They came back announcing they had hidden the flares in the haystack with trip wires stretched out on each side of it. The approach was covered, the flares were buried in the stacks, and if anyone came that way and hit the wire, we would get a real display.

"That's all we need," complained someone in the captain's party. "Burn the guy's property; maybe burn down his house."

"Go back, move the flares away from the stacks," the two were ordered over their protests. Griping that it was always dangerous to retrace your steps in the field and that the flares were hidden along the most likely approach, virtually invisible to anyone looking for them, the two went back and put the flares on the other side of the path four or five feet away from the piles.

While the flares were being repositioned, a series of whispered debates on whether the flares should have been moved traveled around the perimeter. The pragmatic argument—that our lives were worth more than somebody's house or drying thatch—seemed to carry the day among the bait. The officers, it appeared to many, had a different view of the relative worth of their troops' safety and that of a stack of straw. A few defended the move. But the decision had been made, and the debaters did not get a vote.

With whispered jokes all around about just what medal the captain would get for throwing himself on a flare to save a pile of straw, we set up for the night. Rather than lie in the mud, two of us tried sleeping sitting up back-to-back with rifles laying across our laps under our ponchos. It worked. Right after a "Thank God the straw is safe" from my human back support, I fell asleep.

It couldn't have been more than fifteen minutes when someone tapped me on the shoulder and whispered, "Movement. Everyone down." I passed the word to the new member of the squad, now sleeping back-to-back with the person next to him. More information, coupled with best guesses, slowly found its way up and down the line. Someone on guard thought he heard or saw movement in the vicinity of the hootch where trip flares had been planted. But the overcast skies cut down the available light for the starlight scope to magnify, and it couldn't be confirmed. The captain, Alpha Six, consulted with the other officers. Their decision was to send up a handheld illumination flare in the vicinity of the movement. Striking the base of the flare against the heel of one's hand sent it several hundred feet into the air, where it would ignite and then float slowly down under a small parachute, lighting the battlefield below. The captain fired. The flare shot into the night sky, lit at its apogee, and sailed under its parachute down to earth.

Now, lying in the water we thought we had avoided for the night, we strained to see anything that wasn't just a shadow of the illumination. The flare continued its downward trip as we tried to focus on constant features of the terrain. Finally, it landed, a one-in-a-million shot, right on the pile we had moved trip flares away from to protect them from being set off. I saw Alpha Six as Oedipus, his actions to spare the pile assuring its destruction. Quickly, the pile ignited. Within minutes, the family was outside screaming, trying desperately to stop the fire.

An hour passed, with the an old man screaming in Vietnamese to his uncomprehending listeners, probably wondering and asking why we burned down his property. A lieutenant who had been sent by the captain to help finally concluded the matter by getting a piece of paper from his pack on which he wrote something and then gave to the Vietnamese man. He pointed at the paper he had written, then at his wallet, and again at the paper, nodding reassuringly. The note's recipient continued talking, pointing at his loss to a departed lieutenant. The lieutenant returned with the answer to everyone's question, which found its way down the line. He had given the man an IOU for "one pile of whatever we burned" and signed it "Uncle Sam."

On future company-strength missions, whenever there was a pause to decide which way to go or how to navigate across a canal, someone would whisper to those around him, "Pop a flare, sir." One family of hearts and minds lost, but on the other side of the equation, a brief, small uptick in company morale.

Sometimes heart and minds were lost at greater cost. The areas we crossed the first few weeks were all new to me, but those who had been in country longer would occasionally recognize a distinctive area where they had been before. The area the platoon was moving through was visually distinctive. Several rows of trees appeared planted with paths intersecting at right angles through the groves. Several remembered it instantly. Doug recounted the event.

"We were here—what?—two or so months ago." He paused, waiting for someone to confirm the date. "The area had all the signs warning of being heavily booby-trapped," Doug said over his shoulder as we moved toward the grove. "You know, the three parallel sticks lying on the ground, three notches cut in trees. Higher came over the net saying that the booby traps indicated they were hiding something. We tried to get some Papa-san to walk point for us through the grove so we could check it out, but he pretended not to understand what we wanted. So this kid—couldn't have been more than twelve—led us through the grove. He seemed sort of excited at guiding us through the trees. VC sniper must have been watching the area. Fired a single shot and got the kid. We rushed him back to his house, called Tan An Dust Off to medevac him out, but he died a few minutes later. They shot a kid because he was helping us, and they wanted to make sure nobody else would. The mother screamed at us and punched and slapped at Doc, who was carrying the boy. Crazy fuckin' war. They shoot a kid who probably sees it as playing a game. The mom blames us, I guess, because we involved her boy in the war. These hearts and minds we aren't getting."

The trouble was, there was no good choice for the Vietnamese hearts and minds. The corrupt South and its love for money and status and privilege, or the totalitarian North and its disdain for the worth of the individual. Those poor families who shared their tea with us during the day, who welcomed the Viet Cong into their houses at night, and who were forced to give their sons to one side or the other deserved better.

My friends back in the world owed the boy's family at least a little honesty about the nature of the Viet Cong.

CHAPTER 11

Enlightenment at the Listening Post

While their cargo was out walking in the sun, the armored personnel carriers—the ponies—remained circled in a defensive position where they had dropped off the company, which had changed from mounted infantry to infantry. The driver always stayed with the pony, as did one or more from the platoon. We were not privy to whatever determined whether that number was one or more.

Whatever the rationale, I was staying back with the ponies tonight. I watched the company move out, the new guy who had joined the squad a week earlier in my usual position. I would be part of a two-man listening post outside the perimeter. At dusk, two of us were to move to the intersection of two dikes about 200 meters from the circled tracks and then alert those on the tracks of any movement we saw or heard.

We were an early-warning system. In the jungles of much of Vietnam north of us, a listening post would look for a thicket of grass or bushes to provide concealment. You could not see them, but you could hear anyone coming through your area. If you found the right spot, they could not see you either. If traffic came through, you would report it and then decide if it was better to wait it out or start moving back toward the perimeter. Usually, the best bet was to stay hidden and wait to be called in.

Here there was no concealment except darkness. You found a dike running parallel to your perimeter and settled there.

With darkness settling in, my partner and I moved across the paddy and onto a dike a little over 100 meters from the

tracks. We were told to go farther out. The next move positioned us almost 200 meters from the tracks and 150 or more
in the other direction to the wood line. There were no bushes
or plants to hide in. The terrain was open rice paddy for the
200 meters back to the tracks and almost that to the wood lines
in front of us. As we settled in, he pointed back at the tracks,
whose shapes I could make out against the night sky behind
us. Keep your head down as much as possible, he told me.
"Your head isn't all that different from a VC head."

I turned and whispered, "How do we get back inside the
perimeter if there is an attack?"

He shook his head. "Best we wait it out, hoping like hell
nobody comes through close to where we are. If they do and it
looks like they're coming through close to you, just throw
grenades in their direction. If you shoot, your muzzle flash will
give our position away. Throw the grenades, then follow me to
the nearest intersection. We got to keep hidden from them
without getting hit by our tracks firing our direction."

"Basically, we're screwed," I summed him up.

"Basically."

We settled in. The soft FM voice in the night called to us.
"Lima Papa Two. Lima Papa Two. Sitrep uptight, break squelch
two times. Over." I waited for the call to me, then depressed the
button as requested. Fifteen minutes later, the voice returned.

I depressed the speaker button. Sleeping didn't seem to
make a lot of sense with only two of us, so I stayed up during
both of our watches. As the hours passed, my awareness of our
vulnerability increased. I remembered Donald and Benny talking about a listening post that was almost taken out as mortars
were walked in on the ponies. I strained to hear the sound of
mortars firing or landing.

At daybreak, the listening posts were called in. We took
down the trip flares we had set up and walked back to the
tracks, where I rearranged some cases of Coke to get some
sleep.

Driver's morning singing woke me after a few minutes.
I did not know Driver well. He did not go out with us on

missions, and in camp his priority was working on the track. He asked about the listening post, noting that he thought it was the worst duty.

I agreed. "Not a high percentage choice if anything's going on."

"Yeah. Guess their thinking is you trade a couple of guys on an LP for all those on the tracks." He continued, "Sort of depends on where you are inside or outside the perimeter."

Something in Driver's description of the listening post haunted me as I struggled to capture in words something that only made sense at the level of emotion, words that would help me tell if there was some difference I might or might not be seeing. It meshed too naturally with the machine gun trying to find us a few nights earlier.

For the most part, we found the enemy when he wanted to be found. We had artillery and airpower. We could move troops very quickly. They could not fight us heads up. So they hid and found us when they were ready, for whatever reason, to fight. We had an overwhelming firepower advantage. The way to get to use it was to tempt them into attacking. Since the war was not going to be won by holding a specific piece of real estate, we had to tempt the bad guys to attack some vulnerable-looking unit and then bring our big guns to the battle. We were not killing to capture a town or a crossroads and then move on. We were not capturing their territory.

We were trying to get them to attack tempting targets, targets walking around in rice paddies and wood lines. A few of us would be killed, but a lot more of them would. A few of us were not being traded to save more of us or capture a path. A few of us, but not too many, getting killed wasn't the price of this strategy. It *was* this strategy. We were giving up our lives for the sole purpose of taking more of theirs.

Could it be that simple? Give them the opportunity to hit us so we could hit them harder? Surely, our goal was more than just to trade lives at a rate they will choose not to sustain. "There might be an NVA platoon in this area. If we go in company size, they'll just stay hidden. But if we go in platoon or squad size, they might think they can do some real damage to us. We'll move in a blocking force behind them." And the part not said: "They may hit five in the platoon, but we'll take out twenty-five of them."

Was this just what war is when stripped bare of pretense, war with no intermediary rationale for killing? In our previous wars, it seemed the killing was a means to some other strategic end, taking a bridge or destroying their supplies so they could not fight. Those things could all be accomplished in principle if, per miracle, nobody was killed. The body-count strategy could not.

Whether our body counting was the strategy of the morally impaired or of the brutally honest about what war, all war, finally comes to, it was also the strategy of those who don't know history. The French had already won that war, ten to one.

Meanwhile, the decision theorists on the other side were also deciding how many lives they had to trade before we wearied and went home.

"Cheese," Donald had once called us. Cheese it was. A trap won't work without it. But cheese was one up on us. It doesn't know it is cheese.

The second night, I stayed with the track, pulling guard with Driver. It seemed like a better way to fight a war, sitting behind a quarter of an inch of steel with a .50-caliber machine gun in front of me. The following morning, we picked up the platoon after their two-day mission. I tossed beers to the squad as they passed backpacks onto the top of the track. I had missed them. As they began telling their stories of the mission, Driver turned his head back to me.

"You gotta write about all this someday."

"Nobody'd believe it," Benny said as he handed me a belt of ammo and climbed on top of the track.

"That's why he's got to do it," Driver said.

Benny nodded. "You gotta do it."

Mission finished, we headed home.

CHAPTER 12

Small Things and Big Things

I found myself adjusting to the physical rhythms of war. Out for a few days and then return the base camp for an overnight. At Binh Phuoc, we would first clean our weapons and then search for a shower that still had water. Five or six waking hours were then ours. I fell in with the letter writers. Squeezed into the enlisted men's club, we would pass around cheese puffs or potato chips, reading letters from and writing our letters to those back in the world.

"Damn," I said. "This is a letter to my mother, and I sound like you guys. Listen to this. I've mentioned 'AOs' and 'Lumo rounds' and 'sitreps' and even '*even*.' She probably hasn't understood anything I've written to her since my first week here."

"Nobody has understood anything you've said since your first week here," came a voice from the next table. "And that's when we quit listening."

Conversation danced from topic to topic. We replayed the last mission and started or repeated rumors about the next.

Some fell in with the dopers who chose to spend their moments in camp high. Some tried living on the boundary of the two universes. Other than saying, "Keep it out of the field," I didn't judge. I knew I hadn't yet earned that right. Each found his own way of coping. I did not know what help I might eventually need in the next ten months or nine or eight.

The field, too, had its routines. We humped most of the day, more and more in squad rather than platoon size as action in the area slowed in recognition, we assumed, of the now-arrived monsoon. In the field, we would blow bunkers that we found, and there were always fresh bunkers to be discovered. Occasionally, we would spend half an hour out of a late afternoon's sun in some family's mud and thatch dwelling, usually one large room. The head of the family would come in from the field. We offered cigarettes or candy. He would offer tea, reusing the same leaves as the afternoon wore on. After an hour, we were drinking hot water. For half an hour, we would do the hearts-and-minds thing while a squad leader would take a two-man reconnaissance patrol to select the evening's ambush sites. Then we would return to the war, settling first into pre-night and then moving into the permanent night ambush locations.

Time, the constant, continued to move mercilessly slowly. Twelve months crept into eleven. Eleven months was still forever as was ten, as—I was sure—would be nine. Ninety days of this, and I would have 270 remaining. Even the addition of a new guy to the squad didn't make me feel any shorter. Time's arrow seemed stopped in flight. We took the days as they came to us. There was no other choice.

Meaningful moments were found in the small things. A good day was one when the enlisted men's club had potato chips. When we got fruit in our C-rations. When we took a break from walking and sat for ten to fifteen minutes talking as we got the weight of our packs off our backs. When we found a few minutes of shade. When Donald hijacked a conversation about girls left behind and revealed to us the reason for his unequalled success with women. ("Been a family secret, but you guys are almost family. Polite and direct. You walk right up, smile, and say, 'Excuse me, would you like to do the dirty crank?' You got to remember about walking up to her though. Yell it across the room, and it won't work more than half the time.") When we first heard the tracks coming to pick us up at the end of a mission, knowing that meant a cold Coke or a cold beer. When we had a letter from home.

War, too many know, is a lot of boredom bracketed on each side of a few moments of terror. What needs to be added was that the boredom, too, has its highs and lows. Maybe you have to stand on the terrain to see the contours.

Even watch on an ambush becomes routine. You listen and stare into the blackness, waiting for a reassuring request for you to break squelch. You stare at distorted shadows in front of you, trying to remember if that's how they looked a minute ago. You are both relieved and frustrated at the end of the night when nothing has happened. Maybe it was to relieve the boredom—I am not sure just why—but I had slipped shoe polish and a dark rag into my gear. As I sat there in the dark, I polished my jungle boots. I applied layer after layer of polish, which I buffed between scans of the horizon through the starlight scope. Shining made no noise, but I still stopped every twenty or thirty seconds to listen to the darkness. When the day broke I had boots in the best condition they'd been in since I got them in Oakland. I asked, with feigned sincerity, several people why their boots looked so bad. Word spread. Everybody wandered by to look at my boots.

That I had polished them last night was too stupid for anyone to offer as the explanation. The most common hypothesis was that I had somehow gotten a new pair from supply before the mission. Alpha Company's supply sergeant, like most of his supply brethren, felt it more important to have material on the supply room inventory than out in the field where infantry would use it.

"You think you can get me some web gear. This is going to fall apart," said the new guy.

Benny said, "No let's get some of the stand-down slippers. Nobody in our company has any. Bravo's got 'em."

Two Six would have none of it. Instead of moving out along the dike, he marched us out across a muddy paddy. The shine had lasted less than twenty minutes.

Those were the small things that interrupted the boredom. Small things, but they mattered.

Some days were for the big things. The company stood in formation for a memorial service for members of the company recently fallen in battle. This was the second I had attended in my first month. We stood in the road that ran down the middle of base camp. In front of our formation were the rifles, boots, and helmets of the fallen. To the chaplain fell the task of finding the right words to say to the living, the living who would be killed the next mission or the one after that.

He told us they died honorably. He told us they believed in what they were doing for their country and for the Vietnamese people. He told us they knew the cause was just.

How could he know? How could he know what they believed? I was in their company and did not know what they believed. Maybe they believed in a cause. Some here did. Some didn't. Some refused to talk about it.

I thought of my gear sitting in front of a company formation, the chaplain saying I died for a just cause I believed in. For the moment, all of the anger and resentment I felt about the last six months of my life had only one target, the chaplain. I hated him.

The dead deserved better. Surely, they deserved at least the truth. But even in its most solemn of ceremonies, the army dared not allow a chaplain to tell the truth. He could not say that Smith, unlike Jones, had serious doubts about the wisdom of our being here but still did what his country asked.

If he couldn't tell the truth at this moment of all moments, then couldn't he, shouldn't he, be silent?

A few hours later, still driven by anger, I approached those I had become closest to and extracted a promise I knew they would not be able to keep.

"If I'm killed, go talk to the chaplain and tell him I did not have a strong conviction in the rightness of our being here and had asked that he not justify my death by saying I died believing that I knew the cause I was fighting for was right."

One member of the asked for the same promise from me. I agreed. I doubted if I would have the courage required to keep it.

Everywhere around me were acts of self-sacrifice and courage, disregard of self to help another. Why was the kind of courage truth sometimes requires so hard? How could a chaplain excuse himself from seeking the truth before he spoke? How could I run to help comrades isolated from the company during a firefight, but not be certain that I would ask the truth be told about them in death?

Truth, not willing to be used, demanded I look at myself. Maybe it all came down to this: I just didn't want to be a name mentioned at the memorial ceremony by someone who didn't care whether what he said was true—in a few months to be only an occasional thought for the one or two in the squad who remembered me. No one's story here continues much beyond him. There are too many interruptions. My story here would not long survive me. It would soon begin to flicker, maybe surviving long enough to become the occasion for some new guy's moment of sadness at his own circumstances.

I was afraid that all most of the war's dead would ever be was a lesson for some new guys on what not to do or the guy the old-timers might mention occasionally, the guy from ancient times of three or four or five months ago, what the February new guy had been for me. Beneath the anger and resentment and hatred was an unrelenting, ever-present sadness.

CHAPTER 13

Mouse Ears

Personal revelations notwithstanding, the war went on. A few miles to the east and north of Binh Phuoc, the Vam Co West River forms a double loop to the south before merging with the Vam Co East. On a map oriented south, the double loop would resemble a Mouseketeer hat, explaining the area's polite designation by the officers who sent us there: "The Mouse Ears." But conventionally, maps are oriented north, and that orientation more appropriately described the area to those who had to go there: "The Testicles." It was not considered a contested area. It was, Two Six assured us, owned and operated by the Viet Cong. We were visitors who paid to get in.

The large, lazy loops of the Vam Co East meant large areas of deep mud in and around the nipa palm wood lines. The Vam Co West, with its own double loop, reconverging with the east to form the Vam Co, magnified the effect. Movement was slow and difficult through the mud and nipa palm, made all the slower by trying to avoid the extensive booby traps—usually hand grenades attached to trip wires, but occasionally something larger, a command detonated artillery shell or the Chinese version of the Claymore mine hidden in a tree. There was no way to explore all of it even with several battalions working parts of it. Our operators sent us in hoping they would get lucky and we would stumble across something. I knew none of this on my first trip into the Mouse Ears. I knew that this time we took the south and east road out of the camp through Binh Phuoc village, past the district ARVN compound, and then followed the road to the northeast. I could feel the uneasiness from those who had been here before. "Just a bad area" was the assessment.

The day started badly for the officers. The bridge track, which lays a metal bridge across small canals and rivers for other tracks to cross, encountered some problem which stopped everyone for an hour. That fixed, we were underway for less than ten minutes when a track got stuck in the mud only a few hundred meters off the road. It was an hour of frustration for those in charge, an hour of physical comedy for the rest of us as we watched a series of failed attempts to get a track out of the mud. Sitting around waiting, Doug reminded us, was good duty. "Pays the same as walking through mud. An hour later, they each get you an hour closer to DEROS." So we waited by sleeping, playing cards, walking over to talk to those on another track.

There were those who did not understand the zen of waiting. Several tracks away someone not content just sitting jumped from the top of his track to the paddy, partially clipping a paddy dike with his heel and breaking his ankle in the process. The company commander, having suffered almost an hour of being yelled at over the radio by the S-3, the operations major back at battalion, for getting a track stuck and then not getting it unstuck, started yelling at a platoon leader, threatening to court-martial the soldier with the broken ankle for deliberately breaking his leg to get out of combat. As the medevac helicopter came on station to pick up the injured soldier, a few of those closest to the helicopter jumped off tracks and paraded around with exaggerated limps to the cheers of comrades.

Eventually, the track was unstuck, and since the army doesn't build delays into its schedule, the morning's diversions meant only that once dismounted, we would move more quickly and with fewer stops. Our destination: some place represented by a grease-pen circle on the captain's map.

The first minutes of the route could have been the areas I'd already seen built to a smaller scale. The rice paddies were smaller, and the wood lines were always closer. As we moved deeper into the area away from the road, signs of regular tending of the paddies disappeared. Run-down dikes suggested that many of them were no longer being kept, but small, isolated areas appeared to still be cultivated.

While the oldest of the old-timers had gone into the Mouse Ears several times, nobody remembered the particular area where we stopped early that afternoon. Our platoon's memory, like that of almost every platoon in country, went back no more than that of its senior members. In our case, that meant seven or eight months. That meant walking into many areas where the advice of those who had been there before, who could tell us what we might find, was no longer available. It was the price the army was willing to pay to limit problems homeside. And it was certainly a non-negotiable price draftees were given for the promise that if somehow they could stay alive for a year, their war was over.

The troubled start to the mission, the reputation of the area, and the ambiguous signs of human activity contributed to a sense of dread as we moved into the area identified by the grease-pen circle on the captain's map. Circled were several hundred meters of open ground. Flat and muddy, this open space was not someone's rice field. Crabs scurried about, unbothered by our presence. Nowhere were we more than 100 meters from a wood line. There were no dikes, not even run-down ones, to get behind if someone opened up on us.

An open area like this had to be "zeroed in by Charles's mortars," someone complained.

"Hell, why waste mortar rounds when they can stand in the wood lines and shoot? What are you going to hide behind if somebody opens up? The crabs?" said another.

I was relatively new, but I felt what everyone else felt. This was a bad place. We could accomplish nothing here but die pointlessly.

Yet it was becoming clear from the circulating rumors that the captain was intrigued by the place, by the small open place hidden in the wood lines, and he was going to deploy at least one platoon here for the night. The objections accelerated, but only among those unable to alter the course of events. Everybody wanted to intervene, but nobody knew what to do or say to a captain who needed contact to redeem a bad day.

I wandered over to the area where the radio telephone operators from the captain's party were gathered and singled one of them out. I said, "Hi," and then asked him some questions about his radio. Then I did it. "Hey, has anyone said anything about whether we get a tide in here, and maybe what time? Some of the guys want to know." I continued a few minutes more asking questions about how long it took him to get comfortable on the radio.

His mind was elsewhere. He looked at me. He looked at the mud and the crabs. He excused himself and walked over to the captain. The captain looked at the mud, the crabs. He looked at his maps. Were we close enough, I wondered, that one would show the South China Sea? He got on the radio, I assumed, to ask battalion about tidal washes. He called the platoon leaders over and told them we were moving out. I saw the radio telephone operator looking for me. I kept several people between us, never looking in his direction.

I knew nothing about tides. I just asked a question I had heard others asking. I refused to think that I had done something. I had merely taken advantage of my location to make sure that all options were being considered. Maybe something happened because a company commander did not want to explain to the S-3 how, in addition to getting a track stuck, he had drowned a platoon. Or maybe the captain was not a bad guy who wasn't going to risk lives without better information. But mostly, it was just a matter of people not willing to admit there was something they didn't know and ask someone who might. Within fifteen minutes, word began to spread that we were moving out, seeking some other circle on a map. "Turn those programs to Plan B," Donald said.

The other circle, it turned out, was on the other side of a river, which we reached as the jungle absorbed the last few beams of light as quickly as they found their way toward the jungle floor. Two swimmers stripped down and swam the river, landing about ten meters downstream on the opposite bank. With their end of the rope one had carried with them, they made their way back upstream and secured their end around a tree on the bank. One stayed on the opposite side of the river while the other returned to our side, this time aided by holding on to the rope, which kept him from moving down stream. One by one, we loaded our gear on an air mattress, wrapped the sling of our rifle around our right arm and laid it on the mattress to keep it out of the water, held on to the rope with our other hand, and were escorted across the river by one of several other swimmers. On the other side, we fanned out for security. In a little over an hour, the company was across the river. It was now too dark to move far through this terrain. We formed a perimeter, assigned watches, and settled in for the night.

The talk the next morning was of the mortar rounds some heard being fired last night. I didn't know if I had slept through it or just had not yet learned to identify the *whump* of a mortar being fired in the distance. Nobody heard them land, but a few were speculating that the crabs in our tidal wash were the target. Overnight, several soldiers had become experts on tides, noting that had we stayed there, we would have been standing in three feet of water, unable to get down as the mortar rounds exploded around us.

I knew I had crossed some sort of line the day before. I was equally certain I had saved lives. I didn't want to debate myself any further. I just wanted to stay away from the captain's radio telephone operator. If I had offended the war gods, it would not be that easy.

That morning, we moved out in platoons. More units meant more area could be covered. Alpha Six and his headquarters element joined our platoon, and our route quickly took us off trails and out of open paddies and into the nipa palm. The calf-deep mud in which the nipa palm grew limited our movement to a couple of hundred meters per hour. The mud grabbed at our feet, and extracting one foot just forced the other deeper. Several lost their balance pulling a leg out of the mud, more often than not filling their rifle barrels with mud.

The column halted. Then word filtered back: "Booby trap."

"Doesn't make sense," someone suggested. "Nobody in his right mind would be walking here. Why the hell is it booby-trapped?"

"We're close to something. That's why."

Without resolving the issue, we moved on, each pointing out to the next filament line and the grenade attached to it. Before the last in line crossed the trip wire, we were stopped again. This time, different words worked their way back down the column: "Chinese Claymore in the trees."

Two Six had to make a decision. Assume the worst: it is command-detonated, and someone is watching, ready to set it off. We can't go backward because it would blow as soon as we started to change direction, and we might walk back down our path into an ambush. If we go forward and increase the distance between men to the maximum distance allowing you to see the man in front, we'd never have more than two people in its kill zone.

"Take us on out of here," Two Six told the point after looking at Alpha Six.

As we walked out, each showed it to the person following him, the object hanging in a trees about five feet off our route. Someone did not want us walking through here. Not that it really mattered. Even if we looked and dug for several days, we would have to be just plain lucky to find the weapons or medical supplies hidden here. If we didn't stumble into it, we weren't going to find it. We continued past the Claymore, inching our way through the wood line.

"Son of a bitch."

I looked up to see Donald trying to balance himself on one leg. The other leg revealed a socked foot. His combat boot was missing. The mud had refused to yield when he tried to lift his foot out and had pulled his jungle boot off his foot. By this time, any noise discipline was long broken.

Even Two Six joined in. "That's why your mother taught you to tie the laces."

"Can we leave the boot and booby-trap it?" someone asked.

"Hell, rescue the boot and booby-trap Donnie."

I held his rifle while he pulled his boot out of the mud, shook out the water, and, with someone's help, got the boot back on while standing on one foot. When he moved on, I tried to step around the area he had just stepped in. Realizing how stupid that was in an area that was booby-trapped, I tried to step back. My step didn't bottom. I pushed down hard on the left leg to stop the right, and it kept going, too. In a matter of seconds, both legs were knee-deep in the mud, and I was unable to move either leg. I was stuck. Someone took my rifle and my pack, hoping the weight reduction would help. I still couldn't move.

The barrage of one-liners was now aimed at me. The general theme was whether or not the mud would make a prisoner of my fatigue pants the way it had Donnie's boot.

"If it does," I answered, "every Viet Cong mama-san in the area will *chieu hoi*"—the name for Viet Cong who rallied to the government side.

"Hell, they'll all go back North."

"Hell, we'll all go North."

Finally, two people grabbed me under the arm and, with my feet extended, managed to pull me out. Ten minutes farther down, another soldier was pulled from the mud. It had stopped being funny.

"Get us out of the woods," Two Six ordered the point.

That afternoon, Alpha Six called his platoon leaders. We were coming in a day early. As always, we weren't told why. As we mounted the track, someone reflected on our mission. "One track and three soldiers stuck in the mud and one broken leg. Could have been worse."

"Roger that," came several simultaneous replies. "Roger that."

I continued trying to understand my own intervention into the course of the war. Had I pushed a personal first domino? Or had any significance already disappeared, swallowed by the larger forces controlling our destinies.

"Let it go," a voice, maybe my own, kept whispering. "Let it go."

CHAPTER 14

Super Strategy

Sometimes we were given a reason for the particular mission we were on. We were to discourage a sniper who was disrupting ARVN operations. We were going to keep supplies from moving through a new area. We were to look for any sort of evidence of a buildup in some particular location.

Yet there was a sameness to all our missions, whatever the reasons we were or were not given. We walked around during the day, blew the bunkers we found, looked in people's homes, and then set up ambushes at night. It struck me that there was a single operation type for every type of operation.

I tried to take up the issue when we stopped, but nobody seemed ready to expend the energy that thinking required.

"You're thinking again, man. That's a problem you have, you know?" I was told.

"Saddle up," yelled Two Six.

We started walking. Our conversation—or my conversation—had apparently changed nothing. Nobody seemed to be doing a sniper-finding walk or a find-enemy-supplies walk or even a look-for-signs-of-activity walk. We just walked.

Eventually, we walked through a wood line and into the paddies at a place where the path divided. A sharp new path ran to the left. The old path continued straight ahead. We continued for about fifty meters on the old path and then stopped. As we looked around, we realized how lucky we had been. Our backs were to the trail that branched right. Down the trail stood two bunkers. We had been walking with our backs to two bunkers. Two Six yelled my name, and I moved beside him. He drew a route in the air with his hand showing me how I should approach the bunker. I retraced our steps down the path and then stepped off the path and into the paddy about where I thought Two Six indicated I should. I then got parallel to the bunker and walked up to it, my eyes switching from the ground to the back of the bunker to the nipa palm a few feet away. Arriving at the bunker, I tossed a concussion grenade into the open back. I ran back over the last twenty feet I had just covered when the bunker disintegrated. I took out the second bunker the same way, approaching slowly and deliberately, and then as soon as I tossed a grenade, I sprinted back across the ground I had just taken so deliberately. I looked up and saw the platoon had kept moving on while I protected their back side.

In basic training, you could easily spot the country boys who were hunters. They found their way so easily. Every shortcut worked. I was not one of them. Put me in any suburb, I thought, and I will get you through—even if it is gated. But this was not like that. A fear of being left behind was a near phobia of mine. Staying as close as I could to the route I had followed to the bunker, I ran back. I reached the trailing squad as its last man turned the corner. I heard the word pass forward that I was back and both bunkers were out

I began to feel hot and weak and assumed it was my run. As we moved on, I knew it was more serious. I told Doug, who told Two Six. Within ten minutes, some Delta microbe showed me its strength relative to mine. The attacks of diarrhea occurred in ten-minute waves. Two Six moved me into a small house to get me out of the sun. A young boy had apparently been designated by his mother to show me where to go whenever I had survived for ten minutes. Two Six designated Rick to accompany the two of us.

"Two Six," he reported on returning, "when we move out, he's got to be at the back of the column."

The battalion aid station sent a message to keep giving me water. Brigade Dust Off said they could have a helicopter out just about sundown.

Doc, the platoon medic, kept pushing pills and water at me. Finally, I fell asleep, to be awakened by the sound of helicopter blades on the other end of a conversation. I told Two Six I was all right, that I could walk to pre-night, and I was one more rifle in a firefight. Two Six agreed, but told Doug not to give me a watch that night.

A voice a couple of positions down asked, "Hey, man. If something happens to you tonight because of you being sick, what are we supposed to tell the chaplain? Are you for or against diarrhea in time of war?"

Two Six, who was unaware of my problem with the chaplain, started to ask a question but must have thought better of it. "Alabama, take us to pre-night."

We adjusted our gear and fell into position. With our rifles alternately posed right and left, Alabama took us to pre-night.

CHAPTER 15

The Plain of Reeds

At Fort Lewis, we had practiced exiting a helicopter—more correctly, exiting a wooden mock-up of a helicopter. As soon as the crew chief gave the word, we jumped from the ship. Half the squad would exit one side and half the other side, moving out about twenty feet, forming a defensive perimeter as our helicopter "took off." Jump, run, and form a perimeter. Training lasted about forty-five seconds.

June 27: The 1st and 3rd Platoons had already lifted off. The 2nd Platoon stretched out along a runway at the Tan An airfield, waiting for the flight that would pick us up and drop us off somewhere in the Plain of Reeds, a flat, often swampy open area that ran from a few miles to our west to the Cambodian border. Here the foe, old-timers agreed, would be mainline units of the North Vietnamese Army. We sat quietly. Some caught a few minutes' sleep. There was little of the usual premission joking. There was little conversation. Most sat staring at nothing in particular.

As I waited, it seemed that I saw news traveling toward me. Groups of two or three or four people became animated and then passed the excitement to another group. Nerves fired synapse to synapse until the organism itself had the information.

The visual had the panicky feel of a phone ringing late at night. I hoped for whatever was the equivalent of a wrong number. The feel was appropriate. The 1st Platoon, the second platoon to air-lift out, was in heavy contact and had taken casualties. The first platoon out had been picked from its landing zone and moved to the firefight. We would be the third in.

The 1st Platoon had taken fire almost immediately on approaching its landing zone. They were setting down near a wood line and started taking fire about fifteen feet off the ground. They took fire from NVA who disappeared into the scrub grass only to reappear somewhere else. The platoon finally found cover behind a small dyke, tried several times to attack, but each time was driven back. Well-camouflaged and well-constructed bunkers simply were not vulnerable to rifle and grenade fire. Two helicopters took runs at the wood line, but rockets hitting nearby did not affect the bunkers. Two South Vietnamese jets came on station and put a 250-pound bomb right on one of the bunkers on its second pass. The bunker disintegrated.

That's what we were heading into. For several of us, this was our first air-mobile, the term of choice in the 9th Division for helicopter assaults, and our landing zone was hot. Then the news got worse. The lead platoon had several KIA.

Our flight arrived at the Tan An airstrip. We climbed on knowing we were going into battle.

Under different circumstances the flight might have been enjoyable. The air rushed through the open chopper, and for a few minutes, we were actually cool as we headed out on a mission. Occasionally, a tracer round fired from the ground would bend toward us. The door gunners would return twenty or thirty rounds to the apparent point of origin.

"Jump, run, form a perimeter"—repeating the mantra would help me, I thought, from screwing up. Saying it also kept my mind from focusing on why I needed to say it. "Jump, run"—I was interrupted mid-thought.

"Two minutes out," someone prepared us.

Despite trying to get my bearings as we approached the battlefield, my brain simply could not. Then I tried to get my bearings as the helicopter approached, but my brain couldn't organize the rush of data it was receiving. The helicopter banked in. The fleeting images of changing terrain, of earth, then sky, then earth, moved too quickly to provide a lasting portrait. Trees and fields not very far below us now changed too quickly for us to do anything but wait to be pushed off the helicopter. How long had the pilot been flying in order to be able to reference his landing zone from his constantly changing perspective? Empty shell casings were spit out as the door gunner fired his machine gun at something hidden somewhere.

"Go! Go!" someone yelled, slapping my helmet. I slid to the edge, looked down at the six-foot drop, and jumped. Running and forming a perimeter would have to wait. Conservation of momentum was first in line. The extra weight of my pack wanted to continue forward. I wanted to stop. Physics won. My feet stopped when they hit the ground. The rest of me kept moving until my face slammed into the ground.

Hoping no one had seen me, I got up and sprinted fifteen feet, hit the ground, and stared into the distance in front of me. I could hear the battle but see nothing. I looked down to my left. There was the new guy who had been sitting by me on the helicopter. We acknowledged each other, and then he turned back to staring into the terrain in front of us. I looked to my right, but nobody was there. I tried to think my way through it. Either I was the company's right flank or the person on my right had been hit—or maybe something worse.

Words trying to make themselves heard above the fight. "Back here." Then: "The other way." Were these words for us? I wondered, then felt a panicked recognition that they were. Someone was yelling at me. I looked back in the direction I had just come from. Slowly, the meaning of what I saw struck me. The battle was all to our rear. We had jumped off the helicopter and run away from the battle. The entire company was back there, thirty or forty feet away and facing the other direction. Jump, run, and form a perimeter, except when the enemy is in fortified positions in a wood line and all in one direction—yours. Two of us had done it by the book. We needed a new book.

"Come on," some sergeant I didn't recognize motioned. Giving up the ground I had just conquered, I crouched and ran to his position. An old, worn-down dike gave us ten to twelve inches of protection from the enemy in a wood line fifty feet away. He told me to get down as low as possible, that we had artillery support on the way. It arrived.

The ground shook as round after round smashed into the wood line. Breakfast rose in my throat. We were close enough to the impacting shells to catch pieces of mud and wood that were thrown by every explosion. A large dirt clod hit me in the calf of the leg extended behind me. "Curl up!" the sergeant yelled. I fought an urge to argue geometry. Lying on my side, curled up, or stretched out—my exposed area should be nearly the same. I curled up. Dirt and debris continued to fall on us as round after round rearranged the bunkered wood line.

Some continued to collect and manage information. At the other end of the line, they needed a poncho for one of the bodies, and one had been seen near where I was. One of the few who had carried a poncho that day, I handed mine over.

Trying to reunite with my squad, I crawled to someone I recognized from another squad in the 2nd Platoon. He had already learned some of the details. The initial platoon came under fire as soon as the helicopters started to land. Some of them were still ten feet in the air when they came under fire. A soldier who had been standing and returning fire had a rocket-propelled grenade take one side of the upper half of his body. He was the one they needed my poncho for. The others were killed by rifle shots. One of the dead was in his second month in country.

I tried to understand someone who would stay standing while returning fire. Get prone. If possible, get lower. Then return fire. Was I more prudent, or was he just more brave? He had been killed, and it seemed wrong to ask about the wisdom of what he had done at that moment. Another thought was not deflected. I had arrived in country within days, maybe the same day, as someone who was now dead. I could have been in the new position in that platoon. "Stop thinking," I screamed silently. Then, for the moment, the questions were buried.

Word was passed around: Get ready to move back. We're bringing in air strikes.

We moved back about 150 meters from the wood line to an indentation, perhaps part of an old canal, that stretched for several hundred feet before disappearing short of a small wood line to our left. That wood line ran for 100 feet to our front along our left flank, blocking any view of what was to our left. To our right, as we faced the enemy wood line, was open ground. The company reassembled into platoons and squads, and then, with orders to keep our heads down, we opened fire. Thousands of rounds of rifle and machine gunfire did little real damage to bunkered positions but did ensure that nobody would be moving. Even staring into the wood line, I could not make out a bunker.

I had been feeding belts of ammunition into Benny's M60 machine gun, clipping belts together, and keeping the belt lined up straight. His usual assistant gunner had ended up somewhere else, reappearing just as we stopped firing for the coming air strikes. I rolled away and let the assistant gunner slide in to the left of the gun. Two Six walked down the trench and came up behind the three of us. He spoke to Benny. We were exposed on our left. Someone needed to anchor that side of our line and make sure nobody came through the trees on our left. Benny and his assistant sprinted the hundred feet and disappeared into the wood line.

The air strikes arrived. Bombs blasted into and around bunkers. Then another flight. I watched what looked like a keg of beer fly low over our heads and then erupt in flames in the wood line. From more than a football field away, I could feel the heat of napalm. Keg after keg exploded, searing the contact area.

The battle obscured any sense of time. Had we been here minutes? Hours? Air strikes were followed by small-arms fire, followed by helicopter gunships, followed by artillery strikes, each pouring its kind of death into the wood line we would eventually enter. A resupply helicopter dropped off more ammunition and C-rations. The pounding of the position continued through our lunch. Artillery barrage after artillery barrage, jet pass after jet pass continued against their position.

Two Six found me and said that Benny would need more ammunition. "Take them a canister of belted M60 rounds."

I headed to the resupply area and picked up a canister of belted M60 ammunition for Benny's machine gun. The wood line that had swallowed him was 100 feet beyond the end of our line and meant crossing about that much open terrain and then finding wherever they'd positioned themselves on the other side of the wood line. Parting words from my mother, long hidden in the layers of memory, found that moment to emerge: "Don't ever take a chance you don't have to."

"Sorry, mom," I whispered and ran in a crouch to the wood line.

I yelled out their names as I approached the trees. I got an immediate response. The stand of trees on our left was only twenty feet thick. Benny and the assistant gunner were in a water-filled bomb crater.

Bomb crater! Slowly, it sunk in. *Bomb crater.* This battleground was not virgin. One small part of the war's secret was reopening itself. This spot mattered only for the killing that was done here. No other strategic objective except killing. Kill as long as each side was willing to pay the price. A year of simultaneously being hunter and hunted. A year of activity that would have no bearing on the outcome. A year as Sisyphus.

Who had died the first time the war visited here? The second?

I joined them as we waited, waist deep in our private wading pool, on the next round of artillery.

We were out of contact with the rest of the company, and as far as I knew, only Two Six knew we were here. But for the moment, we were content to stay in a crater. The war would not yield that moment. Above us suddenly was the flapping sound of a helicopter rotor. It hovered while the crew tried to make out who we were. From above, we were bodies in a tree line a couple hundred feet from the main unit. We couldn't yell above the helicopter's roar. It pulled out to the side, and the door gunner strained to see into the darkness as he kept the machine gun trained on our vicinity. We could see them much more clearly than they could see us. "What are they going to tell our families if they shoot us themselves?" the assistant gunner tried to joke.

The stalemate couldn't last. Independently, we took action. Benny put his hands in the air, saying we had better surrender. The assistant gunner joined him. I had slipped out of the crater and was crawling to the edge of the wood line when the rotor wash opened a spot in the branches. The gunner saw Benny's surrender and made him as one of us. The ship started to bank away. I had been crawling with my thumbs up as I inched toward the open space, assuming my hands would be the first thing to appear. Benny's surrender had gotten their attention. As the ship lurched, I rotated my wrist and replaced my thumb with a finger that wasn't doing anything at the moment. The helicopter lurched, then glided away. We settled back into the crater.

"That gunner was the meanest looking little guy I've ever seen," Benny said.

"Roger that," we said together.

The middle three or four hours of the day had been spent softening the position. But we knew the steel and jellied flame raining down on the North Vietnamese in that wood line were only our temporary proxies. Eventually, we would have to go in there ourselves. Mid-afternoon turned out to be the appointed hour.

We were told to rejoin the platoon, and we found our way to the area where they were assembling. We worked our way to the east, approaching parallel to the enemy front. If we had disrupted their communications, they would not see us on line until we were fifty feet from the front edge of their position. We waited on one last battery to fire into their position.

Then came the command for the 2nd Platoon to take the lead. It was our turn.

We walked through the other two platoons that would follow us in. They spoke soft words of encouragement or gave us a thumbs-up. Their eyes revealed something deeper, gratitude that it was not them. I would have felt the same. One held a camera above his head and took pictures of the battlefield we were entering.

On line, we walked past the few inches of dike that had been our protection that morning—probably what kept the first platoon in from taking even heavier casualties than it had taken. I strained to take in everything: signs of still-hidden bunkers, movement, spider holes. We kept moving forward. Forward into the outer edges of the wood line, a landscape now rendered surreal by the hours of destruction dropped into it. My brain couldn't do anything with the information my senses were providing. Trees were uprooted or chopped in two. Patches of grass untouched by our efforts existed ten feet from an area where nothing survived. It was taking all my energy to try to make sense of the landscape. There was nothing left for interpreting signs of possible danger. I shook my head and tried to imagine what a surviving bunker would look like. No image presented itself. I tried again to take in everything as I waited for the bullet that would speed from a bunker or from someone hidden seconds earlier in a spider hole. Ten more feet. Then ten more.

I heard my name called from behind. Then shouts of "Pull back" registered. I looked to my left, and the person there was running back out. Only four or five of us remained in the wood line. I had been too focused. All of my brain's ability to represent the world had been locked in on the twenty or thirty feet to my front. I looked quickly for a sign of anyone who might not have heard. I turned and followed the rest.

We would never find out why we pulled out. A quick cost-benefit guess? Some other unit would go through the position? A desire to avoid being counterattacked by other NVA units that would collapse on this area after dark? A random number generated by a computer in the basement of the Pentagon? I had my own theory. Six weeks earlier, Senator Edward Kennedy had done something that was almost certainly widely discussed among the military's political caste. He went after the army on strategy, for sending the men of the 101st Airborne online into bunkered positions at "Hamburger Hill."

The implication was obvious. The U.S. Army was the British officer corps of another war, sending young men to greet the rounds of machine-gun fire. It resonated with me.

But for whatever reason, we were being pulled out.

So we ran, without looking back. A helicopter flight was picking up one of the platoons as I tumbled into a crater where the rest of the squad was gathering. To the right of the ditch where we had spent much of the day, we were a football field and a half away from the wood line as we waited. A second flight arrived, picking up another platoon. Last in, we were to be last out.

A familiar sound. Then another. Whistling noises over our heads. We reached the conclusion together. "Taking fire," someone shouted. We lowered ourselves below the rim of the crater and listened to the isolated shots sail past.

I didn't understand the enemy. Tons of steel ripping through their position all day. Napalm sucking the air from their lungs. We were pulling out. It was over. They could just wait. Instead, they were inviting us to again join the battle.

It was just a few bullets fired at the end of a long day. If we would listen, they were telling us something. Our enemy was different from us. They had to believe in what they were doing. Sure, a part of it could be they were firing because they were angry and this was payback and somebody was ordering them to fire, but nothing else made as much sense as the simple fact they were true believers. They hated us. They would not give up. They would not accept a compromise. The war would go on until they could no longer wage it.

We were the last squad to slip onto a helicopter for the ride home. Those from the company we never saw in the field, the first sergeant and assorted people from the company rear, shook our hands as we moved through the company area. We killed twenty-four of them, we were told. I wondered how we knew. Nobody would take note of the sniping as we pulled out.

The next day, they grilled steaks for us. Lunch was mid-morning since we would be moving out that afternoon. I wrote home and subtracted one from our side's casualty count. The battalion commander spoke and told us it was an old enemy, the 1st Independent NVA Regiment. Expecting a shout, he told us, "And we beat the crap out of them. That's one whole platoon of theirs that this morning they discovered were missing." The awaited cheer did not come. Our officers turned around and stared at us, and where they caught someone's eye, there was momentary applause and then an "All right" from the owner of the wayward glance.

It seemed strange to me to say that it was "our" old nemesis, the 1st NVA Regiment. Their membership had probably turned over almost completely in the last year and a half. We, too, were not the unit we were fifteen months ago. Whatever 2/47 had done in defense of Saigon during Tet of '68 was not part of our motivation for fighting today. How good they were had no effect on how good we were.

At the awards ceremony, they gave Benny a medal for holding an isolated position and protecting our flank against a bunkered position in the Plain of Reeds twenty-three miles from Saigon. Except for the platoon leader whose platoon was hit in the opening battle and who had earned his medal, the officers got medals mostly corresponding to rank. The company commander got a Silver Star.

At the ceremony for the American fallen, the chaplain talked of the ultimate sacrifice they were willing to make while knowing of the rightness of their cause.

One of them had been in country since May. Who decides?

CHAPTER 16

Marijuana Wars

I had never seen anyone use marijuana out in the field, and it would be hard not to notice anything being done in the field. Except for the two-man reconnaissance patrols that were sent out late each afternoon to locate an ambush site, nobody was out of sight of everyone for more than a moment or two at a time. That left two groups. Some would get back to Binh Phuoc and disappear until it was time to head out the next day. Never particularly large in number, they were essentially fighting the war with the equivalent of a constant hangover. The other group was made up of those who sought a little assistance in coming down after a mission. It was not a priority with them, and if they missed a stand down or two, it did not really matter. These together constituted about a third of the platoon. The majority of the platoon was the "never had" and the "had once or twice, but were finished with it, and did not intend to try again." I was in the latter of these two groups.

And there were reasons to believe that the use was not one-sided. Reasons like the marijuana patches found growing in NVA-controlled areas or the reports of long-range reconnaissance patrols that observed small groups of NVA soldiers smoking during their off time.

The track mechanic who went into field with us had been given a name by Doug. He was Mechanic, pronounced as if there was a four-letter first syllable and a one-letter second syllable: MECH-a-NIC. He was responsible for my first and only pot use. He had been pushing me to give it a try. War is an occasion where the "you may never get another chance" argument seems particularly compelling. I yielded.

Nothing was particularly notable from the inside looking out. I was not more relaxed or, as far as I could tell, more or less anything, except perhaps a bit more talkative than usual. Mechanic asked, "Now what exactly is it that you studied at college? I never made it quite that far." Just saying "philosophy" would not be an adequate answer, so I talked about Plato's story of the Ring of Gyges, which made its wearer invisible, and what he would do differently if he had the ring and knew he would never be caught. I then brought up Plato's Guardians and the manner of their upbringing and compared it to a democratic society, where, in theory at any rate, the defense of the country should be the duty of everyone.

Other than the fact that he really seemed to enjoy it, we had different pictures of what had gone on. I thought I had set up a couple of classical philosophical problems that he enjoyed. For weeks, he went around telling everyone what neat stuff I studied in college and they should try to get me to do my college rap.

Two One Pony during the six months
a year it was covered with mud.

Below: First thing on returning from
a mission: clean your gear.

Robe the Strobe, squad leader.

Benny usually carried about 200
yards of linked ammunition on himself for the M60 machine gun.

Below: Al, Larry, and Alan. Behind
Al is his guitar.

Tracks moving into night laager
before platoons move out.

The author standing on the perimeter of Binh Phuoc.

Below: Smitty. Most people shower
when it is still light.

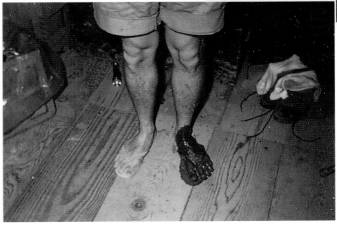

The S-1 tries to avoid having his
picture taken.

A mortar cache found hidden near Binh Phuoc.

Below: A little celebration on 2/47's next-to-last night in Binh Phuoc. Left to right: the S-1, the battalion XO, and the S-3.

The large rice paddies of Long An Province. The tree line in the distance marks the river.

Al Ford standing by battalion head-quarters.

Below: A change-of-command cere-mony for 2/47.

The only clean track in the Delta. A former Playmate and a Dean Martin dancer attracted a lot of attention when they visited base.

Taking in a show.

Below: The Tan An Bridge.

With pre-night approaching, units all over the Delta will be moving to or settling into pre-night locations. In about thirty minutes, they will move to permanent night positions.

My corner of S-1 for writing and processing awards and decorations.

Above: Water buffalo.

Typical hootch.

Rick and Donnie (probably) on *Two One Pony* as pre-night approaches.

Tracks of the Americal Division in Tam Ky, March 1968.
U.S. ARMY

Below: A track in action, August 1968. U.S. ARMY

A pair of tracks, with tanks in the background.
U.S. ARMY

CHAPTER 17

Rach Kien

Rach Kien was perhaps twenty-five kilometers to our northeast on the other side of the Vam Co. It was home to an infantry battalion, the 5th Battalion, 60th Infantry, which shared its base with South Vietnamese military police. The fencing separating the two units suggested the Vietnamese were not completely trusted. We were to be there for two weeks, reacting to intelligence reports of a planned attack on the base. We were to patrol part of each day and then return to the base to eat before we set up squad-size ambushes at night. Several hours on most days would be our own time. There were new ways to spend it. We were not allowed in the town of Binh Phuoc. Rach Kien, however, was an open town.

"Harry's or Lefty's. Maybe Harvey's. Something like that." Doug tried to remember the name of the town's main attraction.

The first day started out well. While a couple members of the squad engaged someone on guard duty in a conversation seemingly to gather information about the area, I walked off with a cot from their guard bunker. I wrote several antimilitary slogans on it as proof it was mine should anyone ever challenge my rightful ownership. Someone then added a Snoopy head to it. I threw it on the track.

Then to the mess hall for an early-evening meal before our mission. Our first ambush was squad size, and the squad, for the moment, was down to seven. At dusk, we left the base, walked through the town, and then into the countryside. It was clear we were to be trip wires to alert the base that the bad guys were on the way and maybe to slow them down for a few minutes. Not the best career move, Donald advised.

But once again, Doug had come through. Five hundred meters beyond the edge of the town, he led us to a small garden plot, perhaps twenty by twenty. We set positions at each corner, looking away from the town. We covered perhaps a 240-degree sweep and, with a glance over the shoulder, a full 360. We were elevated a foot or so above the surrounding rice paddy, which meant someone would have to be standing or at least sitting up to fire a round into our position. It also meant we weren't lying in water.

"Three-hour shifts," Doug announced.

I felt the touch of someone trying to wake me up, but when I looked, no one was there. I thought I saw movement, paused to see if I could make it out, then found the selector switch on my rifle and eased it off safety. Someone was moving around the garden. I moved toward the center of the garden. Someone suddenly sat up two positions down from me.

"Rats," someone whispered.

"Rats!" echoed someone else.

We were not the only ones who found the position attractive. The rodents ignored us. The garden had better to offer them, and for the moment, we were merely obstacles to their movement around the garden.

"Any chance they'll turn on us with all the vegetables around?" I asked. I checked my zipper. Nobody knew. Nobody slept. We waited for light and our return to base.

We were in camp for only a couple of hours when we were sent out on a short patrol. We spent a couple of hours walking in the sun along one likely approach to the base, and then we returned to Rach Kien, where I discovered the cot that I had gone to all the trouble of stealing was missing. I found it under a sleeping soldier from another platoon. I woke him and told him he had my cot. He denied it. Several from his unit gathered around to defend him. Not a big thing, but a cot was one of the bigger small things. I wanted my cot back but didn't want to be shot. The alternative was to rely on military discipline, the chain of command. I found his platoon sergeant and reported the theft. He quickly dismissed me. I thanked him for his time and asked where I could find his platoon leader.

"Damn," he said. "What do you want?"

"My cot."

"How can you prove its yours?" I described the Snoopy head, inviting him to compare it with those on all the other cots in our squad. I added that some previous owner had written what I thought might be antiwar slogans on it.

Over the protests of those gathered around, the platoon sergeant ordered his man to give up the cot. As he reluctantly did so, he pointed out all the things written on it, demanding to know how I could write that crap: "Let's win one for Gipper-san!" or "How many Vietnamese fought in our civil war?" I had a lot to say, mostly about how there were two thoroughly rotten groups of Vietnamese, neither one of which deserved to govern, and how the people lost no matter which side won. But I said none of it now. I took the cot and walked away through mumbled threats of revenge.

Donald stayed behind and talked to the other squad. When he rejoined us, he described how he had explained that the cot had belonged to my best friend who was hit a month ago; how he had always joked that if he got wounded, I was to take care of his cot until he got back; how I got a little crazy about the cot but was otherwise an all right guy. He reported back that the platoon sergeant rolled his eyes, but the rest of their platoon seemed to understand.

With the cot secure and the afternoon free until 1700 hours, the discussion focused on Harry's entertainment center. Apparently, we had seen the place the night before. As we had walked through town last night on our way to the garden, a man appeared in a darkened doorway. "Get the damn VC tax collector!" he yelled as we walked past.

We stopped by the MP station at the main gate. Anyone going into town had to show dog tags and a condom. We made our purchases, listened as we were told we were AWOL if we weren't back when the gate closed, and then headed into town.

The prospect of two weeks in Rach Kien was taking on the appearance of good duty. Ambush at night. Half a day of patrolling. Half a day back at base camp. And we were about to discover Harry's.

Left at the main gate (where the MPs checked to see if we had our dog tags and a condom with us), into the town of Rach Kien, through the doorway where the man stood the previous evening imploring us to get the VC tax collector, past the outer room where older soldiers nursed drinks to country western music, and into the inner sanctum. We found our table as the bar girls found us. For some reason, I had expected the sophistication and worldliness of Elizabeth Taylor in *Butterfield 8* but was greeted with adolescent giggles—but giggles from masters of manipulation. The squad bought their time with an uninterrupted convoy of drinks. Periodically, led by the hand, GIs from around the bar would leave for a yet more interior room.

"You pretty boy," one girl told Donald. "Make beautiful babies. I souvenir you." She led him into the back room. "Souvenir him? Why him?" our looks asked each other. We concluded it was his youth. After all, one of the girls had at some point called him "Baby-san."

Superstition growing, I resolved to say no today. I feared I had tempted the gods of war too often of late with my actions in the Mouse Ears and even with the cot, and I needed to even up the ledger. Harry's would be here tomorrow, and maybe tomorrow I wouldn't feel so far in debt. I quickly decided on my plan, which would be so low key no one would pay attention

Her courtship ritual was brief. "You want make boom-boom?"

I looked at her sympathetically, and then, in my best Vietnamese from the dozen phrases I had memorized, I told her sorry, I was feeling a little sick. "*Dinh cai dau,*" I said, pointing at myself.

The girls at the table started giggling and then spoke excitedly to other girls at nearby tables who all looked my way.

I gave a puzzled look to my tablemates. "I just told her I was a little sick."

"Not quite," a just-returned Donald said.

"You told her you were a little insane," Doug corrected.

Half an hour later, he told us it was time to get back to camp. As we prepped for the night, a delegation from another squad walked up. They singled me out. Finally, one spoke, "Sorry to hear about your insanity, man."

"Don't worry about it," I nodded. "Turns out it's not the dangerous kind."

An uneventful night on a platoon-size ambush and then a patrol the next day.

Accompanying us on the patrol were four of the military police who shared the camp. Most of the patrol was along dikes in open paddies, but when one dike led directly into a trail through a small wood line, it was clear this had been our objective. The column stopped for a minute outside the wood line. The Vietnamese National Police bolted from the formation and took up a position behind a dike twenty meters from the wood line. Someone was sent to talk to them. They shook their heads in reply. They were not entering the wood line. They stayed together, peering over the dike.

I tried to be charitable. They were in it for the long haul, and this piece of real estate wasn't worth the risk. The less charitable perspective was reinforced when we glanced at them as we slipped into the wood line. They wanted someone else to fight this war for them. They could not miss the contempt in our eyes. But they knew if they stayed out they would be alive tomorrow. One more piece of the zen master's neverending puzzle? We were allied with the Vietnamese who did not want to fight against the Vietnamese who were pretty damn good at it. Had we been choosing teams for PE class, the teams would have been quite different.

The present moment demanding my entire attention, I put the questions away. The moment announced itself quietly, the explosion muted by the vegetation. The squad leader from

Alabama had hit a trip wire connected to a hand grenade. Leg wounds they didn't think were too bad.

The trip wire was all we found that day. After the medevac, we returned to Rach Kien.

There are some constants. The shower assigned to us had no water. I went looking for another, found one, and washed off a layer or two of the day's grime. I was soon joined by our company commander, which meant I was in was the officers' shower. Should I just admit I didn't know this was the officers' shower or make a point about the troops having no water? I wasn't forced to decide. Alpha Six didn't recognize me and began recounting his morning's patrol. Naked, you can't tell the officers from the enlisted men.

A night in the base camp at Rach Kien meant a relatively easy night of guard duty for the squad. It also meant we would be able to attend the show their battalion commander was putting on for his men. We had it on good authority, one of the cooks, that there would be nudity. We arrived half an hour early and found the first five or six rows of seats already occupied. We moved into the closest available chairs. It started to rain.

The rain lasted about twenty minutes and was hard enough to drive those around us out of their seats and to whatever cover they could find. We looked at each other and continued to sit and wait. We weren't going to lose these seats.

The show began with Asian bands playing rock tunes as go-go dancers in miniskirts and boots danced on stage. After an hour, their battalion commander made his way to the stage to the shouts and applause of his men.

He talked about what a great job they had done and then said he had arranged something to show his appreciation. He then turned the stage over to the last act, a stripper. The good authority had been correct.

Walking back to the track, we reflected on the day. Someone added it up. "On the plus side, we were able to verify that one dancer was female. On the negative, the Alabama squad leader was hit. And on the negative side, Carr saw Alpha Six naked. A memory he'll cherish always."

The next night was our last in Rach Kien. Our two weeks there became four days. As always, we got no explanation. Our last night, we were to set up an ambush on the other side of town from where we had set up the first night. We stopped near an outdoor terrace of a house on the very edge of town. It turned out to be the house of an ARVN officer. The location gave us a view of the road and the open rice paddy. The officer came out and talked to Doug for about twenty minutes, and then Doug informed us we had been invited to set up on the terrace.

When the ARVN took off on his motor scooter ten minutes later, we considered moving. Robe nixed the idea. Only seven strong, we were too vulnerable to move at night through open paddies. We rearranged our positions so that our rear was covered.

Minutes later, we heard his motor scooter approaching. He was not a Viet Cong sympathizer. He was a businessman. Riding on the back of the scooter was a Vietnamese woman.

"A hooker on an ambush," somebody marveled. "Crazy fuckin' war."

"What time does she have guard?" I asked. "And does she know how to break squelch?" Still ruled by the superstition of the moment, I volunteered for the first guard.

That next day, we left Rach Kien.

CHAPTER 18

Doc

A platoon medic was always called "Doc." Our Doc had just received news over the radio from battalion headquarters. Doc had become a father. Mother and child were doing well. Two Six said to take ten in recognition of this occasion. Doc passed out cigars and candy, and Two Six warned against smoking the cigars out in the field. "The smell will bring out every VC in the area. Wait until we get back to Binh Phuoc." The ten-minute break was spent congratulating Doc and adding up to nine on our fingers.

A few minutes later and we were back exploring an unusual and ominous area.

Doug came up with it first. "The wood line! It looks like a haunted forest from some German fairy tale." We stared at each other, not comprehending, and then, one by one, we saw Doug was right. We could do nothing but agree. It was a haunted forest with a single path leading through the paddy to the wood line.

Doc, who had been a couple of places ahead of me in line, dropped back to right behind me. "Sorry, Chuck," he said, "but I'm taking the medic's prerogative here. I've got a family waiting for me and only a few more weeks with you guys to be back with them. This is a buku bad place."

Two Six called the platoon to a halt and kneeled for a while. He called his squad leaders up. "There's a wood line with no green growing. It's all grays and browns."

"Herbicide?" asked one.

"I'd bet on it," Two Six answered. "For the sake of any children any of us may have, I recommend we avoid the Enchanted Forest. And for our own sakes, we've got to move into a new position quickly. This is just the sort of place he'd go because he knows we won't. Let's not give Charlie a chance to maneuver around and force us into a fight on his ground."

The real news of the afternoon was Doc being so short with us. It was news that led to the first real hostility in the platoon. Our new medic was a conscientious objector who would not be carrying a weapon. Medics were usually given carte blanche with respect to what weapon they carried. Our current Doc carried a .45-caliber automatic rifle. Knowing it wasn't very accurate, I had asked him why he chose to carry it.

"I'm not going to hit anyone more than thirty or forty feet away, but anything I do hit is going down and staying down. The VC will come after any area where we have got wounded collected. I use it to protect the wounded first, but any one of us I keep from getting wounded because I shoot one of them first is better than treating him, and it costs Uncle Sam a lot less."

Doc had always seemed to be one of us. His replacement was something new.

Donnie was as angry as I had seen him. "One less weapon puts us all at that much more risk. It takes away a gun if we have wounded. We shouldn't have one less gun on line just because of something someone believes."

Someone brought up what was certain to be the new Doc's defense of going weaponless. "He's going to say in his defense that his job was looking after the wounded."

Several jumped in to reply. "What if there aren't any wounded? Aren't we being asked to protect him when he won't do it himself?"

The sentiment was almost unanimous. "And how is he going to help wounded when they have been moved to a dust-off area and he's the one there to protect them? The NVA is going to try to take out your dust-off area and slaughter those who can't fight back. They'll sacrifice a lot of men to do that. If you were wounded, wouldn't you want someone defending you who had something to take some of them out? Don't see how it is an advantage to the wounded."

Our new medic came to the platoon within a couple of weeks. Few were willing to speak to him, and he would never try to break the ice to talk to anyone. I tried to talk to him a couple of times, but he was not willing to engage in conversation. "I know what you guys think of me, and I'll live with it." I tried to get him to talk about his religious views, but he told me that he "did not have to justify his beliefs to anyone." Too soon, perhaps, I gave up. He was going to have a long and lonely six months with the platoon. That did not appear to bother him.

CHAPTER 19

Letters Home and the Swimming Hole

The ongoing rainy season brought with it a slowing of activity by the VC and NVA units but left our pattern of activity unaffected. We continued our routine of two or three days in the field before coming in to dry out overnight. We would move out early tomorrow. "Two or three days of good duty," Doug believed.

I sat on some cartons of Coke in the track, decided to whom back in the world I most owed letters, and quickly penned two almost identical letters, each describing two recent missions to fill the family in on what I was doing. I quickly jotted down a few sentences about a mission in the middle of nowhere during which a ten- or eleven-year-old boy walked up on our pre-night position selling Cokes. If he had managed to follow us at twilight without being seen, how hard would it be for an eighteen-year-old big brother to do the same? If he had seen us from some hootch or bunker, so could the older brother and his squad. We knew we were in for a particularly anxious night. Had he tailed us, or had he just seen us? And what was he doing out there? Had he been sent to count us and note our exact location? He was not the local Coke distributor. That much we were pretty certain of. We forced him to leave and then watched him melt into the darkness. The move to permanent night couldn't come too soon.

We never heard anything more about the Viet Cong Coca Cola Bottling Company.

I then turned to an earlier mission and again wrote the account twice.

The second mission I described was a company-size walk through an area new to me. Nobody remembered either seeing or even hearing of it. Our route took us past a pair of mansions protected by an eight-foot rock wall that surrounded both houses. Curiosity got the better of us, and the company walked single file through the houses. Furniture that I knew I would never be able to afford was piled in the center of a large room. A twenty-foot ceiling held a six-foot chandelier. Dozens of curious Vietnamese watched from shadowy corners or dark doorways Dozens of Vietnamese watched us make our way through what was now the dwelling of perhaps five or six families.

As we left the house and headed for the gate, the game was speculating on the history of the house. We debated hypotheses that were really wild guesses. Apparently, the Highers in the company were also curious, and the word went out for anyone in the platoon who could speak Vietnamese or French.

"Sorry, Two Six," I said when he asked. "Only a little German and a little less Spanish."

Nobody in the company could speak Vietnamese or French. An officer in the command group asked me to ask one of the Vietnamese about the house in German—just in case. As best I could I asked who had built the houses. Then I apologized to him in German for our rudeness, just in case they understood.

I added that I felt that somehow the story of the Vietnamese war was the story of the morning's encounter writ large. Sixty or seventy people walk through your house—to them, how could we be anything but another generation of French.

I added a selection of "How are you?" and "What's going on?" questions to one of the letters, sealed it, and addressed it to my parents.

I took the remaining letter and added a brief account of a third mission. We were moving as a company. I now shared the general anxiety our platoon had about company-size missions. Despite the extra firepower we had available to us as a company, it seemed that if something went wrong, we were moving as a company.

The company was moving slowly, stretched out for seventy-five meters along a dike, when those in the column suddenly started tumbling domino-like off the dike and into the paddy. Within seconds everyone was crouching behind the dike. Someone was sent forward to find out what the point element had seen. We waited, staring into the darkness until the outline of steel helmets against the background explained to everyone what the first off the dike had seen: we had walked into an ARVN ambush site, and for some reason, they hadn't initiated the ambush.

A great deal of time went into clearing areas of operation. If there were going to be other friendlies, each unit should know about it and should know approximately where the other friendlies might be found. One of the two of us was in the wrong place. Each side stared at the other for half an hour before some Higher solved the problem by having us move. We walked back to a road and out of the area, passing an ARVN unit displaying three Viet Cong bodies with too much enthusiasm. Occasionally, a report of the ongoing argument between our company commander and the ARVN district adviser over who was in the wrong place would work its way up or down the column.

When I finished that letter, I addressed it to my sister. My mother was still angry that I had not taken one of the ways out that might have been available to me. I trusted my sister with what to do with her letter.

Donnie was the first in the platoon to ask me. "You are a college graduate, aren't you? What are you doing here with us grunts?"

"In fact, your personnel file says you have one year of graduate school," added Two Six.

"Dyslexia," I answered. "Couldn't follow the green line to the blue line and get off on the red one, and never knew what to do if they crossed."

Benny shook his head. "We're not letting you out of this one."

I yielded. If I could not tell it straight with these guys who could I tell it to? "I got the sign-up-for-officer-candidate-school-or-warrant-officer-school pitches in Basic and AIT and even at Dong Tam. I've been waiting four years for this war to end. Not going to give them a year of my life because maybe it will end in the next six months. And it's not obvious either of them has a better chance of survival. Two close friends went into military intelligence. That was the closest I came to signing up. Canada was never an option for me. Somebody else, probably someone with less money or opportunities, would be drafted if I avoided it. I couldn't let someone go in my place, go because I got out. The result is a mother who is angry at me for not taking another way. She even arranged for me to get into the Coast Guard. My guess is she must have met you guys somehow and figures I'll be better off with anyone else. Selective Service let me finish my first year of graduate school, and then I was drafted."

Doug stopped the conversation. "There she is." The good duty Doug had told us we would get was two nights of guarding the engineers who were either building or destroying something near a wide, slow-moving river. It took less than twenty minutes after our arrival for someone to strip off a shirt and walk into the river. Within minutes, almost everyone was in the river, moving easily against its slow current. Water fights and dunking quickly followed. We were thirteen-year-olds on the playground.

I had temporarily escaped an attack by moving upstream when those coming after me started pointing upstream. Someone was swimming off by himself. Probably just exploring to see what was beyond the bend in the river. Unable to get his attention by yelling, we set off after him. Not a great swimmer, I fell behind and stopped. I looked for them and found them fifteen meters in front of me swimming furiously for the bank. They pointed to the bank for me. Expecting to see a Viet Cong company, I looked up the river at what would end the day's play. A Vietnamese village whose houses bordered the river started right past the bend. Behind every hootch, extending over the river was a latrine. Our swimming hole was the village sewer system. We spent the rest of the afternoon watching the river from the bank.

We were kids. Whenever the opportunity to play arose, we took it. A few days earlier, we had gone out with some UPI reporters who had been writing about that part of the war that wasn't often heard about, war in the Delta. They wore fatigues, which, with their hair two or three inches longer than Benny's, led to their being called our hippie squad. We had been told how important a good impression on them was—although none of us could figure out just why.

We circled the tracks, and the three platoons of Alpha Company took off for the war. The slightly muddy ground would make it softer, and thirty seconds later, a football was being tossed around, and everyone was ready for a game. We quickly chose sides. On the first and only play, Mike, who was back at the tracks, ran the kickoff around the end and right by me. At that point, thirty minutes after leaving the tracks, the company returned from what was going to be a three-hour patrol. Nobody knew why they returned when they did. A month later, someone reported that the story on the war in the Delta featured a picture of troops, half of them skins playing football surrounded by the tracks. The caption was something to the effect that tracks circle up to provide security for soldiers playing football. Alpha Six was furious.

Doug got his shot in. "I understand you guys were awful, that Mike ran through you. Remember, we went out to make a good impression. You may have cost some officer a medal."

I was beginning to see a pattern. If it was play, they would stop it after about twenty minutes. That's what we had gotten for football earlier. That's what we got today got for swimming.

As always, without explanation, the guard duty for the engineers ended, this time before we guarded anyone. No word on why. The military's warnings against spreading rumors miss the point. Information is a commodity. The rumors fill the void caused by a lack of official information. And the rumors tended to be more accurate than official word passed down the ranks. The rumor: back to the Mouse Ears.

CHAPTER 20

Two Six

I did not want to be here. Nor did I remember anyone who was saddened by receiving orders sending him home. War is never good, but I had to admit I had been fortunate in my first months. Contact had been infrequent. I was comfortable with the other people in the squad. I was comfortable with Two Six. He had kept the platoon quiet and hidden during his by-the-book take-out of the machine gun. We all felt he was not here for the glory. Nothing is permanent, I reminded myself. Luck can change.

Two days after leaving Rach Kien, we were back at in the Mouse Ears, this time to patrol as squads to cover more territory. In one hootch, we came across a young man of fighting age. Knowing we had to suspect he was VC, his parents tried to indicate he was deaf. Doug told us, "Keep their attention on you," as he worked his way around behind the suspect. After a minute or two, Doug stepped forward and screamed in his ears. He didn't react. While we were not completely satisfied with his innocence, we did not want to hold a detainee overnight. We found our way to the rest of the platoon and moved to pre-night. The night was uneventful.

We moved to the pickup point, and Two Six gathered the platoon around him while we waited for the tracks to pick us up. "No easy way to do this," he said, then told us he had been reassigned and we would be getting a new platoon leader. I had never forgotten his words to me on my first mission. "The object is to leave this place the way you came in." We felt he really meant it. We all knew there was little likelihood we would find another who we thought would care as much about us as about medals or career advancement. Eventually, the questions arrived to breach the stunned silence.

"Why?"

"Is there anything we could do?"

"It just is," he explained, "the army way."

He would be working with the ARVN, and we would be getting a new lieutenant in the next week. He left us with the most pointed advice he had ever given about being alert every minute. "There are people out there," he reminded us, "who want to kill you for no other reason than that uniform you're wearing."

The tracks arrived, and we rode back into base in silence. We realized this could be the last time we ever returned from the field with Two Six. We entered the base, and he was gone from our lives.

We were told the next day we had earned some road duty. We suspected that we were being given a few days for the new Two Six to meet and assess us. Losing Two Six made it a frightening time, but road duty was road duty.

The road we were to guard ran from Binh Phuoc to Tan An. Binh Phuoc was the capital of a district in Long An Province. Tan An was the provincial capital and the location of brigade headquarters. Highway 207, the road between Tan An and Binh Phuoc, was a one-lane dirt road that until about four or five months ago was mined almost every day. It was one road of dozens in the country designated "Thunder Road" by those who traveled them.

The 2nd Platoon's four tracks would be positioned at equal distances along the twenty kilometers of Highway 207 between Binh Phuoc and Tan An. We were told to stay a couple hundred meters off the road in order to have enough time to react to anything that might happen on the road or anywhere behind us. Two of us were to be on guard at all times, one watching the road, the other the rear. At night, we would pull duty as a reaction force at the Tan An airfield. Someone would always monitor the radio. In the morning, one track would accompany the military police as far as Ben Luc on their way to Saigon. And we waited to meet and assess the new Two Six.

My first day on road duty, I read *Catch-22*, a book a psychology professor had urged on me several years earlier. Biting satire, Professor Allen had told me. It read differently in a war zone. Realism, I concluded. Maybe even non-fiction.

What was clearly non-fiction was what we had been told to expect from the monsoon that found us as we settled into road duty. A sunny morning quickly darkened, and rain driven by forty-mile-per-hour winds drove all except the two of us who had watch inside the track. We tucked our ponchos in everywhere we could to keep them from being picked up and blown off by the wind. Occasional bursts of wind threatened to carry us off the track. I tucked and shrunk myself into the smallest surface I could make of myself. No longer needing to spend my energy to keep from being tossed off the track, I was able to concentrate on the Lash Larue impression the rain was doing where it could find my exposed parts. Individual drops were blown hard enough to sting as they landed.

Then, as quickly as the storm had gathered, it dissipated. We returned to our sunny morning. An hour later, the sky had darkened again. The two now on guard were relearning our lessons yelled up to them as we sat inside the track. Unbothered by the rain, from the door on the back of the track, we could watch the world outside lighten up. By noon, we were facing our third storm. As the storm approached we noticed for the first time that the storm was actually a series of storms. The eastern sky was a black-and-white rendition of a peppermint stick, the alternating shadings of dark and light perhaps twenty miles apart as far as we could see.

It was no use moving during one of the downpours. Anyone bold enough to challenge the stormwall would walk with his head bowed, seeing nothing more than the ground three or four feet ahead of his boots. Every minute or so, you would stop, kneel down, and pull your poncho hood as far forward as it would go as you sought information on the world outside.

Eventually, those trying to move against the storm would be forced to their knees. Trying to move in squad size or larger would have you either all sitting together or spread out enough to be ineffective as a unit. Walking with the wind was not much better. Gusts would periodically force us to take several quick, tiny steps to maintain balance, often not succeeding.

As soon as this moment of the storm was past, I put my poncho on one of the stone tombs scattered through the area so that it could dry out before I put it on again. Terribly miscalculating the time between the end of one assault and the beginning of another, I was soon chasing my poncho toward Thunder Road. Everyone gathered on top of the track to watch and to bet on which of us, poncho or me, would get to Thunder Road first. Rick and Driver were exchanging military payment certificates when I returned with my poncho.

Rick said, "You should have tried harder, man."

The second night of road duty, in a hangar at the Tan An airfield, we met a new member who had just been assigned to the squad. His story for why he was joining us now sounded wrong. He claimed he had been in country several months, assigned to an artillery unit. He had asked for a transfer because he didn't like the artillery and he had seen our unit somewhere, and we seemed to have it together. Benny and I exchanged skeptical looks.

"Bet his old unit got rid of him. Volunteering for the infantry was his way of avoiding punishment for something," Benny said when we were able to get alone.

We were assigned times to be awake monitoring the radio in case we were needed somewhere. In the background, we listened and fell asleep to music and news on Armed Forces Radio. I caught only fragments of a story about an incident that had happened earlier with Senator Kennedy.

Several hours later, we were all awakened by Doug's voice. The new guy had fallen asleep during his radio watch. Doug was in his face, yelling that he could get everyone he was with killed. When Doug left him, the new guy tried to approach me.

"I wouldn't ever sleep in the field. Here it doesn't matter since we were just monitoring the radio. Don't mean nothing."

Failing to get the support he wanted from me, he turned to someone else for vindication. I went to Doug. "We have got to get rid of him. If you don't figure out a way, I'm going to quit the war and go home. What are you going to do then if you need someone to make a difficult ankle shot?"

We continued road duty with our new squad member.

Road duty provided the occasion to acknowledge another of the unintended social costs of war. On day three of road duty, a young Vietnamese mother walked up to our track carrying a child, asking for cigarettes and other sellable items. Someone gave her a four-cigarette pack from his C-rations and told her to *didi mau*, get out of here. She stayed by the track, talking to us in broken English we had trouble understanding. She cried once. Then telling us she was not a short-time girl, she offered herself for $5. She hadn't done "this" before, she sobbed, but needed to feed her child. We stared at her not knowing how to react. I started to suggest we give her some more cigarettes and then force her away if she wouldn't leave when the new guy mumbled, "Why not?" He grabbed her and took her to the other side of the track. A few minutes later, he was screaming for her to get out, refusing to pay her. "She's a pro," he insisted. "She lied. I shouldn't have to pay."

"She's a mother, you idiot. You think she kidnapped the kid to scam GIs?" Benny asked.

He wouldn't listen to arguments. "She lied about the product. I shouldn't have to pay," he insisted.

Donnie whispered to me, "Shouldn't he have to return the product to get the refund."

The woman continued half crying, half screaming until finally Benny just insisted, "Pay her."

He wadded up and threw two dollars her. She gathered them up and needed no encouragement when I pointed down the road.

For the second time, I went to Benny to talk about him. "He's bad for the squad. He's going to get someone killed. In the time I've been here, he's the only one I wouldn't want beside me."

That night brought news which buoyed the new guy. He made sure I knew. "Yeah, she tried the same thing with the next pony down the road from us. Told them she wasn't a short-time girl, but needed money for her baby. Same song, man. I knew it. I knew it."

We were pumping unheard-of amounts of money into the Vietnamese economy, money for those who had the right skills or the right political connections, money that drove up the price of everything, making those without access even worse off. How many fathers or mothers looked the other way, not inquiring into how a daughter was feeding the family, making ten or twenty times what the father made? How many husbands? How many ARVN widows saw no other choice? How many Thunder Road girls had the war created?

CHAPTER 21

The Steak House at Binh Luc

Binh Luc was a strategic town, essential to the southern defense of Saigon. It was the Binh Luc bridge that General Westmoreland was talking about when he told the 9th Division's commanding general during Tet, "If the Binh Luc Bridge is blown, you had better be on it." More important, it was the home of the Binh Luc steak house. Doug had us set up to escort the MPs on their morning run to Saigon. At the Binh Luc bridge, they waved us off. They proceeded to Saigon, and Driver delivered us to the steak house. One member of the squad was assigned to wait in the track and make sure nobody approaches it. He would switch off with someone later. We ordered our steaks, and talked, mostly about the soon-to-arrive steaks.

There's such a thing as being too reflective. I don't know why it occurred to me, but it did. I had been in country for just over two months. In that time, I had never seen a cow. Prices at the steak house were awfully low for imported beef. Maybe this was the best bargain in Vietnam. Maybe they had access to the provisions sent to generals. Maybe there were deeper possibilities I did not want to explore. Nobody would want me to ask them to play Guess What You Are Eating. I said I was not feeling good and would take the track and send the guard in. He could have mine.

"It's not the insanity coming back, is it?" someone asked.

The talk about the steaks at Binh Luc continued for several days. They went out of their way to tell me how good it was. Eventually, I knew I would find the right moment to ask them the last time they saw a cow. Just in case they needed any help with the appropriate logic, I would be there to help them draw appropriate deductions.

I was not to get that honor. Someone else had already asked the squad the right questions, and the squad had drawn the conclusions. The next day was filled with speculation about just what we might have eaten.

CHAPTER 22

Changes

Several weeks earlier, we began hearing that the other two brigades of the 9th Division were to be the first units pulled out of Vietnam. The 3rd Brigade, which included us, would be left in place. Except for the fact that they, not we, were going home, the news meant little to us. It seemed not a part of our lives.

That changed. Soldiers from the first two brigades whom some formula declared not to have been in country long enough to go home with their units began transferring into our brigade. Then those from our brigade who had been in country the longest started getting orders. They would be transferred to, and go home with, one of the departing units.

Doug had somehow come into the possession of a new harmonica and had started teaching himself to play. He repeated the exercises endlessly, claimed to notice great improvement from day to day, and assured us that by the time of his DEROS, he would have it mastered. Doug, with almost ten months in country, was the first in the squad to hear. He would be transferred to another battalion a few days before its departure date and go to Hawaii with it. Robe the Strobe was going home.

The prospect of his departure worried all of us. There had been some close calls, but the squad was approaching six months without losing anyone. We attributed that fortune to Doug and Two Six. We worried among ourselves after the Plain of Reeds when he wanted to fire the light antitank weapon he carried into the wood line. He overshot the wood line by at least 100 meters. But he was gifted at the point. He found every sign, every blade of grass bent the wrong way, every bit of discolored vegetation arranged too carefully. Even when he pointed something out as he showed us where to step, we sometimes failed to see what we were stepping around. He was the one we were expecting to do something about the new guy before he got us killed. Doug was going to get us through the next two months. We had thought we would have him at least for that much longer.

Everyone with nine months in country would be going home. We all feared an outsider would be brought in. Or a shake-and-bake sergeant fresh out of school with no time in country. Neither would be shaped by Two Six. Neither would be Robe the Strobe

The changes were not finished. Those in the division with nine months had been slated to go home. Nine became eight. Eight became seven. Everyone in the squad considered Donald his best friend. Donald got his orders. He would be going home. The news was a body blow that expelled the last bits of hope from me.

Joy and pain had become paired particles. We shared in their joy in going home, but their leaving forced those of us left behind to face what we had found ways to hide momentarily from ourselves—how long, how very long, we had left. Left without the ones we had come to care about. Left without those who helped make it possible to face each day. I knew that the squad would never again be what it had been. When Donald told me he was going, I felt alone, as alone as I had felt on the first mission where I stared into a future that would reveal none of itself to me. Again I stared into the abyss. What stared back at me was an unrelenting sadness.

I could see that same sadness written on the faces of those from the other brigades with three or four or five months spent in country who had been sent to our platoon. Because they had not been in country long enough, their units would be going home without them. They were being sent to new units where they knew nobody. Their friends were leaving. They were being ripped from the support they had built in their own units to become the new guys somewhere else, once again the outsiders. Not able to play again the role of the new guy earning his way into the squad, many withdrew into themselves with their only companion a DEROS date. The changes that brought happiness to some mixed that potion with some measure of pain.

Christianity promises us rest. Zen tells us there is no resting place. Late in the summer of 1969, the world did not reveal a resting place.

CHAPTER 23

New Two Six

Our new platoon leader started visiting the squads the last few days of road duty. All we had were reports from the other squads since he had yet to visit us.

"Could have been he was running it up to see our reaction," Benny said.

"Not *even*. He meant it," countered the new guy. "He wants a medal."

They turned to me. I just shook my head. It was the hottest topic in the platoon. New Two Six had recounted to more than one person the story of an overmatched American squad that had ambushed and destroyed the better part of a Vietnamese platoon before being wiped out by superior numbers. Those guys were his heroes. They were the ones he wanted to be like.

The war had started with professional soldiers deploying in units. Now it was a war of draftees, arriving one by one. Affected by the doubts about the war at home, few draftees wandered into the war hoping to make some heroic sacrifice. The platoon—like most platoons by mid-1969—was split by the war. A succession of business-like, get-the-job-done officers might be able to mold the behavior, if not the soul, into what the army wanted—units that would aggressively seek and engage the enemy. It was particularly difficult to accept in a war whose strategy seemed to be to tempt the enemy into taking a few of us in order to lose a lot more of them.

When the initial shock of Old Two Six's reassignment eased enough to allow it, we wondered what we would do if we got that aggressive, business-like replacement whose troops were there for his career advancement.

We didn't have much choice, Donald had said. "Ya go to the prom and your date didi's—you dance with what's left. It's a prom! You don't spend the evening talking with the guys."

"One really dangerous date from my neighborhood might change your mind on that," said Driver.

"One date pretty well describes your six years of high school," Donald retaliated.

I drifted away from the conversation. I had yet to have that let's-go-find-it-and-do-it platoon leader whose purpose was career advancement. My political philosophy, my war strategy, my tactics had coalesced around two maxims: help your buddies, and survive 365 days. Not that you can control it, but you move the odds a few percent here, a few percent there. The New Two Six was going to undo all those percentage points saved. Soon the majority in the platoon would know nothing of Doug or Old Two Six.

I had been here forever. I still had forever to go. My best percentages were behind me.

Eventually, New Two Six worked his way to our squad. He had seen my records and had talked to his predecessor and Doug about me.

"Would like to train you as my radio telephone operator," he explained. "Figure you'll pick up on it quickly. Current platoon RTO will DEROS soon. I'd like someone who could step right in. Think about it."

The survival calculus tried to kick in. Carrying a radio with a whip antennae extending ten feet into the air, the radio telephone operator was easy to spot. Take him out, and you've degraded communication. And since the officer in charge was always close to the radio, shooting in that area might degrade command. So I'd be a target in firefights and for snipers. Take the job, become a target.

On the other hand, as radio telephone operator, I would never walk point. I would be free from the most dangerous job I'd be called on to do. Nor would I be sent off to blow a bunker. I would always know as much as anybody about what was going on. But the real attraction: get the attention of the company CO and become his radio telephone operator. That meant sleeping at the command post at night. It meant only going on night ambushes when we were company size. With nine months left, I might be able to move up in three or four months.

An increased chance of maybe not surviving for the next three months, but then an increased chance the last six. Such calculations are for $5 bets at a casino. As the stakes go up, the percentages become more obscure. It was quantum statistics, where the conjunction of probability and value is blurred. I might have to try to say no to Two Six. He said to think about it. I didn't have to say it just then.

My short-term strategy was just to enjoy the last few hours of road duty, a strategy interrupted by Two Six pulling a surprise inspection of our track. He griped as inspectors always do, but was finding little to complain about. Then he came to our gas masks.

"Anyone ever used these?" he asked. "Have we ever used gas?"

We shrugged shrugs of ignorance. He picked up one and opened it. A bag of marijuana fell out, landing at his feet. We all danced the dance of feigned curiosity, moving in closer, exchanging what we meant to be looks of surprise.

It was a "what if" question I had overheard last week. If someone wanted to hide a stash on the track, where would he hide it? The answer had been in the masks. No chance of accidentally stumbling across it. I looked over at my questioner who was dancing the dance with the rest of us. Two Six opened the rest of the gas masks but found nothing.

I walked over to Benny. "He wants me to be his RTO."

"Yeah? You interested?" Benny asked

"Don't think so, but I got a little time to decide."

"It'll be a new squad, you know?" he added, letting me know, I thought, he understood if I did. He revealed his strategy. There have to be a lot of slots available. "Get promoted as soon as possible, is how I'm going to play it. I know that won't make it the same."

He was right. It would be. Two Six was gone. Doug and Donald would all be gone. It already felt different.

A rumor added to the sense that things were changing. A presidential directive was sent to the military about the best use of college graduates. My objections did not deter my hope. Decrease the number of middle-class casualties. Weren't many options about where the casualties would increase. Offensive policy. I might benefit. Probably just a rumor.

CHAPTER 24

Battalion Headquarters

Sometimes rumors turn out to be true—or at least one of truth's near neighbors. The college graduates who were serving as enlisted infantrymen in the battalion were being called in to interview. Two positions were now open, and since they were not reading transcripts and test scores, everything turned on an interview. "Not playing to my strengths," I thought.

Very little information was available on what jobs were available. Nobody in the platoon was certain, but the pooled information came to something like this: one job was rumored to involve reassignment to an ARVN unit and experience with a radio-no improvement over my present situation. The other was in battalion headquarters and involved writing. That was enough information to market myself.

I had been in headquarters once, my first day in the battalion. I remembered little of the initial processing, my recollections about my arrival in Binh Phuoc starting with my stroll toward Alpha Company. For my second trip, I would be more attuned to the moment.

On the surface, the squad seemed supportive. There were jokes about me getting the whole squad jobs if I got one. Utterances of "Good luck" were the order of the day, but beneath the surface, I suspected and sensed some resentment. Those more senior felt that they had more of a claim than I did. From those I had been with for a while came the mixed feelings about someone leaving. The resentment might also be premature: only two jobs, lots of eager grunts—I might not be going anywhere. I had decided that if I did stay with the platoon, I would tell Two Six I would like the radio gig. No discernible trail of reasons had led me to that decision. It was as much a decision of weariness as of expected utility. Choose quickly and it won't seem so bad if you choose poorly.

There was one clean fatigue jacket on the track. It was Donnie's. It bore the insignia of the engineers, perhaps liberated from some engineer who had washed it, left it out to dry, and turned his back on it for one moment too long. Or perhaps it was part of the routine laundry exchange. Some well-connected Vietnamese woman ran the base laundry concession. The clothes you turned in to the laundry were not always the ones you got back. Socks were never turned in to the laundry. I learned the first time I turned them in that I had just donated a pair of socks to some cause or some person. I had challenged the woman in charge the first time I went to pick up my laundry. I showed her my slip indicating I had turned a pair in. She kept repeating, "No socks." The decibels accelerated until they reached the ear of a warrant officer who appeared to be spending his tour sitting in the laundry concession with the proprietor. He ordered me out. I told him part of my laundry was stolen and held out the receipt. He ordered me out again.

It was apparent there was nothing I could do. I was powerless. Nothing I did would get my socks back. I departed firing the only weapon at him with a chance of being effective: "You working the black market with her or do you give directly to the Viet Cong? You need to decide which side you're on."

"Get back here, you son of a bitch!" he shouted as he headed around the counter. I kept walking.

I got no sympathy from the squad. "Why'd you give 'em your socks, man? That was really stupid."

About an hour before I was to report to battalion headquarters for the interview, I put on the engineer's jacket. Nervously, I walked around the building two or three times to calm down before entering. "Exaggerate, don't lie," I reminded myself. Someone directed me to a seat while I waited to be called to see the adjutant. I hoped that none of the questions were anything about what an adjutant did.

"Captain Bowes will see you now," a young sergeant told me as he pointed to a corner office. Best military bearing I could muster, I stood at attention, reported, and saluted sharply. "You're not an engineer, are you?" was his first question.

"No, sir. This was the only clean fatigue jacket on the track. Not sure of its origin. Maybe a gift to the squad from some DEROSing engineer." He smiled. The ice was broken.

He asked if I had ever done any writing. I had anticipated the question. I talked about writing, about advanced writing classes, about writing clearly. I talked about typing, summer work keeping books—everything clerical I had ever done. I even confessed that in junior high school, I helped the truck drivers in my father's company keep their logs legal. I tried to talk of all this as if it was not unusual in the world I came from. He pushed me to say a bit more. Having embellished enough, I resisted his efforts to get me to claim more experience than I had. It made what could have taken on the appearance of exaggeration seem like basic clerical experience with the ability to write. I hoped the mechanic had been right that is what they were looking for. Quite by accident, I appeared modest.

The conversation then turned to my experience with the radio. The mechanic had been correct about one being a writing job. I trusted he was also right that the other job was with an ARVN unit. "No, sir, just starting to learn a little. Haven't soloed yet on anything major," I told him.

Within several hours, I heard they wanted me to work in battalion headquarters as a clerk-typist with primary responsibility for writing the citations for battalion medal recommendations. I thought once again about my family, how relieved they would feel.

The elation was short lived. As I walked through the company area, I was stopped by the first sergeant, who told me he was not going to release me for the job in battalion headquarters. "We're too understrength," he explained. It was obvious he was enjoying the moment.

"You can do that?" I asked before realizing I had uttered the words.

"Damn straight, I can. I need to look out for the whole company, not just some college grad's job in the rear. At best, we can let you go when we get a replacement."

I knew it would not be very likely the job would stay available long. I headed back to the squad in disbelief. I told my story. However they felt about my leaving, I had their sympathy for this one. "You can't *even* let him get away with that," someone said. "What are you going to do?"

I had to go through or around the first sergeant. It was a fight where all the power was on his side. Around him was the only hope

War demands that soldiers do what, for most people most of the time, is unnatural. It asks that they kill and, in so doing, risk being killed. Not just risk being killed in the way they do when they get into a car. No, risk it by exposing themselves in order to shoot at people who are shooting at them. Risk it by walking through areas they know are filled with devices designed to blow them apart.

The army does try to make this appear to be rational behavior. Shooting back or charging that ambush or not being hesitant to go after the enemy on his own ground actually saves lives they explain. The conclusion everyone was supposed to draw is that they actually have a better chance of survival by taking certain risks. That begged at least two questions. One: should people be put in situations where they have to choose between several acts, each of which exposes them to a much higher than desired probability of dying? We could just as easily cut the risk by not being where people ambush other people. Two: what's least risky for a single individual—that everyone else return fire while he stays hidden, that everyone else charge the ambush?

Consequently, the army does not rely only on its contention that risking one's life is in one's rational self-interest in order to get people to do things that might get them killed. Rather, it relies on training, peer pressure, and the chain of command as motivational factors. Training is not unlike practice for a sport. You repeat and repeat and repeat certain actions to the point they become reflex. Peer pressure is taught with a blunt instrument. Those in charge look the other way in basic training when a squad or platoon takes action against one of its own. And the army presents itself as a seemingly neverending hierarchy, someone above you screaming through the chaos at you to get up to run. A few are truly brave. But in the end, most of the time, most act because they all believe in their buddies.

My present confrontation with the first sergeant was a war within the larger war, the circumstances of battle, but in slow and distant motion. The job in the rear was, I admitted to myself, a way of staying down while everyone else charged the ambush. I would remove myself from the most dangerous part of the war. To get there, I would have to get past the first sergeant. That this was not a battle determined by projectiles traveling at hundreds of feet per second meant time to think. No reflex moved me here. The first sergeant had said, "Charge," but I had hours, not seconds, to respond.

The peer-pressure leg of the army's motivational machine was also there to be dealt with. If I stayed in the rear, those left in the squad would still go out. Everyone understood when someone who had been in the field nine or ten months got a job in the rear. I hadn't even spent half a tour in the field yet. But then everyone with more than seven months was going home. Robe was gone. Donald was going. Driver or someone transferring in would be senior. I told myself that it wouldn't be the same squad that I was leaving. And anyway, I would be New Two Six's radio telephone operator. Technically, I wouldn't be part of the squad. As radio telephone operator, I would, over time, become an outsider. What had started as rationalization revealed the basis of my choice to me. I knew if I beat the first sergeant, I would take the job in the rear. That is what I wanted from the day I arrived

But first, I had to beat him. He might have yelled, "Charge," but I had to get him to accept that I would not be charging. My attention turned to him.

He had given a reason for keeping me. The company was understrength. That had little, probably nothing, to do with his stance. He did not want me to have the job. Perhaps he thought I hadn't earned it. Perhaps he had someone he was pushing for the job. But I had to address the reason he had given. That might not be enough. I might also need to trump his real reason, whatever that was. The company was moving out tomorrow morning. That determined my timetable.

Just before 1700 that afternoon, I took a position between the mess hall and battalion headquarters. I waited until I saw the adjutant who had interviewed me earlier.

"Excuse me, sir." After telling him how much I had looked forward to working with him, I put my own spin on the "however" clause. I garbled what the first sergeant and I had said. "The first sergeant is reluctant to let me go unless they know they will get a replacement for me from the next replacements. Said he couldn't approve it otherwise."

"I'll get back," he replied.

I headed back to the company area. An angry first sergeant saw me and caught up with me near the supply shed.

"Didn't they teach you about the chain of command in basic training, Carr? You don't just go to battalion headquarters with a complaint. You start at the bottom." He paused. "You'll report to battalion HQ tomorrow morning. Get your gear off the track tonight."

I pictured him brushed back by the inside fastball, a very matter-of-fact phone call in response to his "Need my approval," one that simply said to do what they had to do to work out my transfer. Oh yes, Top. I understood the chain of command.

He had something left. "We sent the request for orders for your promotion through a few weeks ago. Since you're now in Headquarters Company, we will cancel those."

Next to tell the squad and Two Six. On the way, I composed a short letter for home. Again, I felt the need to understate it. "Think I'll be getting a job in the rear very soon. Love, Chuck."

New Two Six already knew. He was in the company area when the captain got a call from battalion headquarters. I told

Two Six that I would have liked to have been his RTO if this hadn't become available.

"Take care of them, sir," I said.

The squad had seemed more somber of late. The joy in things like walking around looking for a decent movie that I had seen the first night was not there. Too many changes too fast. Too much uncertainty about the changes still to come. I announced I got the job. I turned over my cot to one of the new guys. I slept on top of the track that night. I played over and over scenes of those who had meant so much to me. Donnie ordering a pizza over the net while we were in the field. Doug's damn harmonica or his singing out Duda's name, "Doo Dah. Doo Dah." Benny with belts of ammo wrapped around his body, checking his M60 machine gun for the tenth or eleventh time. Cleaning my rifle talking with Super G. Checking in with the voice in the darkness: "Sitrep up tight, break squelch two times, over." Mike—Audie Murphy—in sunglasses shouting as we started a mission, "I don't mind. I'm doing it for my country." An executive officer in a helicopter expressing his frustration at not being able to determine who had responded to his order to have one platoon go check on something with the reply, "Unknown station, be advised all you are doing is breaking squelch." And most vividly, Two Six telling Doug, "Take us to pre-night, Roby."

I was off the line.

CHAPTER 25

Learning to Live in a World of Small Things

In Alpha Company, the rules were clear. In the field, do what had to be done, and in the rear, you would be left alone. Once the mission was over, your time was your own for the next eighteen to twenty four hours. Just be ready to go when it was time to move out again. The rear recognized no time that was yours. I was about to rejoin the army, an army of formations and details and guard duty. It meant daily contact with officers whose careers would be made or broken by their performance in this war. Their performance was ultimately the performance of those they led, and those were increasingly becoming a herd of cats.

I reported to headquarters and headquarters company morning formation, my first morning formation since arriving at Dong Tam. After roll call, four were selected to perform the morning's details. I had expected the morning formations, but had not even considered that there might be details. We were dismissed, and I fell in behind those heading for battalion headquarters.

Perhaps 1,800 square feet and located about halfway down the dirt road that bisected the base, battalion headquarters housed the personnel (S-1), intelligence (S-2), and operations (S-3) sections as well as the offices of the battalion commander (a lieutenant colonel), the battalion executive officer (a major), and the battalion sergeant major. S-1, S-2, and S-3 were overseen by, respectively, a captain, a captain, and a major. The officer in charge of each section was sometimes referred to by the section he led. So the intelligence officer would be referred to as the "S-2." My assignment was to S-1.

The personnel section occupied the entrance to battalion headquarters. Sergeant First Class Thomas, an E-7, the highest-ranking enlisted man in S-1, sat at the desk directly in front of the adjutant's office. He was the gatekeeper. Four other desks were scattered around the office. In the back corner was a mimeograph machine. A single ceiling fan circulated mostly hot, humid air near the ceiling. The central building was wire mesh, with planking that let air flow through without anyone seeing what was going on inside. We so rarely had a crosscurrent in the building that if you felt a breeze, you automatically started putting weights on the paperwork to keep from chasing them around the office.

I was introduced to those I would be working with. All were short-timers who had extended their stays in Vietnam in return for an early discharge from the army. Jim had been at Dong Tam and had extended his tour in Vietnam by two months to get out of the army five months early. He was reassigned here to finish his tour when his unit went home. He was the only one of us who had been trained as a clerk. He spoke slowly, expecting to be listened to. He reminded us repeatedly how fortunate we were to be here rather than at a place like Dong Tam with the constant rocket and mortar attacks. Skip was a grunt, an infantry sergeant who had come to the rear for his last few months. It was clear after a few minutes in the office how respected he was. Skip did not look like an infantry sergeant. In appearance, if you were forced to say something, he was a fraternity president. The other clerk, described to me as the army's fastest two-fingered typist, was not in that day. The senior enlisted man was Sergeant Thomas, a career soldier. Everyone called him Sergeant Tom. His reaction to good news, to bad news, to surprise, or to the expected was always "Well, fuck me."

I would be replacing Skip, who had come to S-1 from Bravo Company, where he had been a squad leader. He told me about the job as he walked me around the headquarters company area. He found a bunk for me in a four-man room in the communications bunker.

Skip, who had earned a Silver Star for valor, told me he had come in to battalion headquarters once before, but said the timing was just not right. His old company needed a squad leader, and he went back into the field. The timing was better his next occasion, and he stayed. Our conversation turned to the Plain of Reeds and the Mouse Ears.

When we got back to S-1, I was given a memo to type and a sample format and then spent most of the afternoon reading the regulations that governed awards and decorations, attempting to learn the match between level of courage and a particular medal and describing the action in the language appropriate to that award. Before the afternoon ended I was given the opportunity to see if I had learned anything. The S-1 handed me a brief description of an action recommending a Bronze Star for valor. Even though it wasn't explicitly stated, I had figured out that particular words and phrases were technical terms that were medal specific. "Risking" was not "disregarding risk." Being under "withering fire" was different from "taking heavy enemy fire." I rewrote the narrative, attaching the appropriate descriptors at the appropriate points. I told myself it sounded good. The work day was ending as I finished it. I put it in Sergeant Tom's tray and hurried to the mess hall before it closed.

I didn't recognize anyone in the mess hall. The 2nd Platoon was probably back in the field, and anyway, I didn't really know if I would be welcome. I knew only those three clerks from S-1 that I had met that day, but saw none of them. Alone. For the moment, it didn't matter. I was off the line. For the first time, I let myself think I might actually survive, then banished the thought.

The next day, my boss, the S-1, went out of his way to praise the narrative I had written for the award the previous afternoon. The first day had been kind. I assigned myself the task of becoming indispensable. I would learn everybody's job. I discovered the Army Regulations and United States Army

Republic of Vietnam Regulations (referred to as AR's and U-SAR-V), and I came back to the office each night to read for an hour or two.

Every morning, several of us would be taken out of the company formation for details, work to do in the company area. The detail assignment was for the morning, and we would return to our assigned job in the afternoon.

I introduced myself to the person I had been paired with as we waited for a detail assignment.

"Go check two shovels out from supply and improve the drainage channel," we were told. The drainage channel was a ditch that ran from the camp urinals along the side the road that ran through the middle of the rectangular camp from perimeter to perimeter. Shoveling the thick, heavy mud from the ditch turned out to be more difficult than either of us had suspected. An hour into the task, we had completed less than five feet. My work partner had been an armored personnel carrier driver, and he proposed we borrow an APC from the motor pool, put one of its tracks in the ditch, and let the spinning track in the ditch with the thousands of pounds of weight on it clear a channel.

Over my objections, he took off, reappearing twenty minutes later driving an APC. He said he hadn't had to go to the motor pool. Some friends had a track out, so he just borrowed it. He carefully eased one track into the ditch. In the next five minutes, he improved about ten feet of ditch, as much as we had done in an hour with shovels. Five minutes after that, the APC was stuck, with one track in the drainage ditch and one on the road. We appeared to risk either undoing the work we had done by driving the track across it or, if we moved past that, tearing up a bridge about twenty feet down the road. I suggested the only logical out I saw. I said he should go report to company headquarters that someone had gotten a track stuck in the ditch we were working on, and we were wondering if we should try to work around it or wait for someone to move it.

"You do this?" asked the platoon sergeant who came by while my partner was on his way to company headquarters.

"I can't drive one, sergeant," I answered honestly.

The company clerk eventually wandered by. I told him I thought the platoon sergeant was considering the possibility that someone got too close to the edge of the road, and then left when he could not get out. For all I knew, he could be considering that. That evolved into the story that found its way around the company. A mechanic went for a joyride and got a track stuck in the ditch. The next day, another detail was assigned to repair the steps over the ditch.

Only a week before, I had been with the squad, laughing at the nightly formation of cooks and clerks in steel pots and flak jackets who would keep us safe. That first week, I also stood in formation at dusk for my first tour of guard duty on the Binh Phuoc perimeter.

The bunkers were behind a cyclone fence that circled the perimeter. Out from that were perhaps four or five rows of razor concertina wire. Each bunker also controlled Claymore mines placed at various distances in front of it. Four of us were assigned to each bunker, with two on for two hours while the other two slept. Guard duty was nothing so much as boring. Seated behind a .50-caliber machine gun, we talked to each other to stay awake as we looked into the darkness through a slit in the bunker that served as a gun port. Somebody came around checking on us periodically, and we called in sit reps regularly to the tactical operations center. After midnight came the first break in the boredom. Several kilometers in the distance, occasional lines of red and green tracers searched for each other through the blackness. Someone was in a firefight. Fifteen minutes later, a helicopter arrived on station, and a continuous stream of red tracers raced downward through the night sky. I watched it the way I would a fireworks display. Death and destruction were eerily beautiful. I felt guilty, a death voyeur. As I climbed down for my two hours off, I noticed half a dozen soldiers had climbed onto the roof of the building next to the bunker. They watched the artists at work in the distance.

At 0600 hours, I dropped my gear in my room and headed for breakfast. I knew there had to be more downside to life in the rear than formations and details and guard duty. I did not have to go looking for it. The unit I was assigned to was called Headquarters and Headquarters Company. I worked in a position that was in battalion headquarters. I was a member of a company. What happened if each wanted me at the same moment? I was an enlisted man, and the company commander was my company commander. At the same time, I worked for someone who outranked my company commander and through whom the company commanders' personnel matters flowed. Skip had given me the thirty-second explanation the first day when he showed me around. Everybody is assigned somewhere, including those who are in a battalion or brigade headquarters. So, in effect, I reported to two people. The adjutant, who oversaw the personnel matters, determined what work I was doing at any moment. My company commander owned the rest of me as long as it didn't interfere with my work in S-1. The guard duty I was pulling was duty assigned to me by the company. I should have asked for the full one-minute explanation. I had no reason to know anything about headquarters units. I was not even sure if I had heard the words "Headquarters and Headquarters Company" together before last week.

I had been told to check some reports that would be coming from each company and to correct typos and spellings if I could. They needed to go to Tan An today. I looked over the first two companies and found a few easily correctable errors. Headquarters Company, however, was in a different format. I put it aside and looked at the reports I hadn't done yet. I reread the instructions, and it became clear that an ambiguous direction had been taken the wrong way. I put their requests back in their mailbox, with a note that pointed out the error, and asked if they could redo it.

The Headquarters Company commander came through a few minutes later, stopping at the company mailbox to see what was in there. He did not take the note saying the work would have to be redone well. "An enlisted man does not tell an officer to do something," he said to me in a voice meant to be loud enough to be overheard. He threw the note down on my desk.

"Sorry, sir. Just wanted to make sure this could get to brigade today."

He exploded again and then, bypassing me, took the paperwork to Sergeant Tom's desk. All the eyes that were watching him turned to me as he went out the door.

"That seemed to have gone well," said Skip, as he walked over to my desk. "You should have talked informally with their clerk-typist first. If they do not want to redo it, then Sergeant Tom will figure out something. You have got to be invisible to the officers whose paperwork flows through here. For some communication consists either of giving orders or taking orders. You look on the other person's collar and then your own, and that is all you need to understand your function in the information exchange."

Skip's advice took care of the future. I had the present to deal with. What about those requests that would almost certainly be sent back by brigade? It was lose-lose.

"You sure about the form?" Sergeant Tom asked. "You sure he did it wrong?"

I nodded. "Yes, Sergeant Tom."

"Well, then piss him off now or piss him off later," Sergeant Tom laughed as he picked up the stack of paper. "The person you have got to please is the one you work for in this office. He's the one who is going to keep you in this job or send your ass back to the infantry. You don't want him signing something that's going to bounce back. Let me try to handle this one."

He put the stack of papers in the middle of his desk. Later that day, he picked up and put down the phone as the company clerk walked in the door. "Hey, James Dean," he said motioning to the clerk-typist. "Your reports were different from everyone else's. Just got off the phone with brigade, and they'd prefer it done a different way. See if you and Carr can figure out how to change them."

I offered to retype half of them for him so we could get them to brigade headquarters that afternoon. He accepted.

It certainly seemed to me that this would be the moment for a different type of officer, one who would have explained, "This note makes it sound like you're giving direct order to a superior officer." I would have learned what I was not supposed to do, but he also could have told me how he would like me to handle any similar problems that came up in the future. Instead, he took it on himself to watch more closely the infantry clerks in battalion headquarters.

Another problem arrived later that week, seemingly from nowhere. The operations officer, a major, seemed to have taken an instant dislike to me. He was not in my chain of command, and having no reason to speak to him, I hadn't. That did not stop him from finding some way to criticize me every time he passed my desk. He would pick up and read the narratives I was writing and pronounce them no good. He could not walk past my desk without making some critical remark.

"No, he just seems to dislike you," Jim responded in return to my suggestion that maybe he just hated everyone. He tried to add some perspective. "Major is a make-or-break rank. A couple of shots at promotion, and their career is over. That said, you're not paranoid. He just doesn't like you."

Enough people observed it or heard from those who had that I knew it wasn't fiction.

"You the guy he's hassling?" I was asked when I talked to the radio telephone operators I knew in the tactical operations center who worked with him daily. "Heard about that." All they could add was a rumor being whispered around that he was sent here after walking to the rear rotor of a helicopter in his last unit, the blade grazing the edge of his helmet.

The harassment continued, and eventually, the psychological warfare started to get to me. Everyone in the office noticed, but nobody had an explanation. He was a major. Nobody knew how to intervene. It got to the point where I dreaded going to the office. I told Skip and Jim something I never thought I would say—that I was considering going back to the field.

I do not know the exact route, but Skip or Jim had said something to somebody. "Stay seated," the battalion commander said as he stopped by my desk. "Your boss says you are doing a good job," he said softly. Without actually acknowledging anything, he made the problem a non-problem for me.

The major glared at me when he walked through the office the next few days, but rarely said anything. When he did, I answered with an unbothered "Yes, sir," or "No, sir." Then, one day, I noticed it was over. It stopped without me ever knowing why it started.

That luck comes in different sizes does not mean it is not luck. I was fortunate. No one had shot at me today. Nobody was likely to shoot at me tomorrow. That was a good exchange for putting up with what, finally, were small things.

There is so much luck involved in war. At battalion headquarters, they send you to Company A, and the guy next to you goes to B. A company commander decides, "The 3rd Platoon will take the first flight today." The smallest change and your future is changed. They say it all equals out, but if it's about the big things, how can it?

CHAPTER 26

Medals: Near-Heroes

The slow-motion pace of time did not change with the move to the rear. Minutes and hours, not days and weeks, were still its currency. Still, with the major from S-3 out of my life, I found that, compared to what I was doing a few weeks earlier, most of the time was full of good moments. I was no longer in the field, and there were a lot of jobs in the rear I would enjoy much less. Of the jobs in the battalion rear, this is what I probably would have chosen for myself. It also kept me aware of the cloudiness war brings to choices. I read almost daily about the very real risks soldiers took for their friends—those who would risk their lives to save someone else, someone unknown to them six months earlier.

But what about those others touched by the act. Would their parents want them to take that particular risk? Would their wives, their children? Selfless acts of courage often meant pain for their families. Did an act of self-sacrifice merely shift the tragedy? Or were our ordinary categories of classification just inadequate for these moments? You make the picture larger. You think of everyone likely to be affected. Would anyone ever act? Ethical codes that allow us to live together day-to-day do not capture the choices war forces on us.

One thing it clearly said to me was how very, very important it is to be as certain as you can that war is necessary before proceeding its way.

Old lessons were reinforced: officers had to risk less than did an enlisted man for the same medal. And there were different standards in different companies even within the battalion. An act of heroism in one unit might not be one in another. Rampant relativism—in the army of all places.

I was spending a good part of every day typing memos and reports and requests for orders, and I was becoming someone to ask if there was a question about regulations—thanks to spending an hour or two each night that I did not have guard duty reading regulations. But my primary responsibility was awards and decorations. When someone did something that merited recognition, an individual somewhere up his chain of command would recommend him for a medal and provide a brief description of the action. I would write the narrative, an attempt both to describe the act and to justify the award; it almost always survived unedited as the description on the award certificate. The office began to notice that my descriptions were rarely changed. Reluctantly, I admitted to myself that I took some pride in that.

My job was to facilitate people getting proper recognition, not to challenge the judgment of their platoon leader or company commanders, but if something seemed out of line, I notified the S-1, who would talk to the company commander.

When the 1st and 2nd Brigades of the 9th Division went home, the 3rd Brigade was put under the operational control of the 25th Division. It was their deputy commanding general who flew in periodically to present the medals at awards ceremonies.

Skip prepped me for my first ceremony. "Medals in order of presentation on a tray. Fall in directly behind the general, who will pin the medal as the description of the action is read. He'll say a few words to each as he pins on the medal."

I found a clean green towel to cover the tray, walked to the Bravo Company area, arranged the soldiers receiving the medals and the medals in the same order, and waited. As the general approached, I fell in behind him.

I remembered the ceremonies I had attended with Alpha Company, realizing that although there must have been someone, I had absolutely no recollection of anyone doing what I was doing, carrying a tray of medals following the presenter. I had become one of the invisible ones.

As Skip had told me he would, the general said something to everyone, asking a question about their emotions at the time or how far away they were from the enemy. He was paying attention to the narratives being read. He was good at this.

What he was not good at was hiding his emotions. Bravo Company had written up their Tiger Scout, a one-time NVA who had changed sides, for an Army Commendation Medal, the lowest medal for valor. His actions probably would have been sufficient for a Silver Star had he been an American. I could read the pride in the Tiger Scout's face as he saluted and held his salute. The general pinned on the medal and then walked on, ignoring the salute. He could not hide the disgust in his own face.

I wanted to understand why. Was it because the soldier was a Vietnamese who had probably killed American soldiers? Was it because he had switched sides? I realized I would never know. That afternoon, I saw the Vietnamese soldier wearing his medal pinned to his fatigue jacket. Clearly, it meant something to him. Maybe that was enough.

There were also unstated rules about awards. "I want you to type this up," the officer, a company commander, announced as he moved past me and into the adjutant's office. He handed me a handwritten paragraph with his name and "Soldier's Medal" at the top.

I quickly got out the regulations and was ready when S-1 called me into his office.

"What do you know about the Soldier's Medal?" he asked.

I quickly summarized what I had just read about heroism that does not take place directly in a combat situation, but still demonstrates an appropriate degree of heroism. I was asked by the adjutant to stay in the office while the story was repeated for me. Last night, the company commander relayed, his company latrine had caught on fire, and he had rushed to the scene and put it out before the fire could spread.

"Well, what else do you need here?" the adjutant asked, staring at me and not too successfully suppressing a smile.

"I think we need more specifics for a narrative, something about exactly how this risked injury to self to prevent injury to others, sir. Something about what would have happened otherwise. What could have happened to the captain."

He nodded, and I left the office as those details were elaborated. I heard "could have spread to the company area" and something about "twenty feet or thirty feet from the supply shed." A few moments later, he stormed out of the office. Apparently, he wasn't going to be put in for the medal.

I didn't know the details of last night's action with the latrine fire. They didn't really matter. Nobody was going to get a medal for saving a latrine. Nobody would want his signature on the request. Had the supply room caught on fire or had the fire been started by an attack on the base camp, I would be writing up a medal now.

As word about the medal request spread among his troops, the jokes followed.

"Saved the latrine from a sapper attack, I hear."

"We can all feel safe knowing that no NVA are going to set themselves on fire and run through our company area."

"Yeah, they might be mistaken for our latrine."

"You suppose it was to create a diversion, or was the latrine Charlie's target all along?"

"Hell, I'm going into business with the captain when we get out. Putting out bathroom fires in the suburbs. Get ourselves a van."

"Well, be sure to put some flames on the van."

"Why wait for the van? Paint some flames on the latrine.

Had he earned recognition for bravery? No, he missed it by at least thirty feet, the distance from the latrine to supply.

CHAPTER 27

New Guys

Days did pass, even if too slowly to be noticed as it happened, and the people I met in S-1 started going home. I would miss them, but not with the hidden pain that accompanied the departure of someone with whom shared combat was the connection. Our words were not able to express the complex attachments and dependencies that develop in the field.

The change marked something larger. A few days before he was to leave, someone asked Skip what he would do if confronted by a protester back home. Skip said he looked forward to it. He would take a swing at the guy.

"I just need a reason for throwing one punch."

I expressed surprise. "Really?"

"I'm serious," Skip said. "Just one punch. What are you going to do if someone hassles you?"

"What I'm worried about," I said, trying to take the conversation elsewhere, "is this 'Make Love, Not War' thing. What if it's either/or but not both? And what if it is not a he, but a she who hassles you?"

Skip held up one finger and mouthed, "One reason," and then took a short swing.

We knew, though, there was something bigger behind the discussion. In 1969, a majority of Americans no longer approved of our presence in Vietnam. We were here for a country that did not want us here. The anger among draftees was turning from the protesters to the government and the military who said they had to be here anyway.

The first to leave was the two-fingered typist. Shortly thereafter, Jim and Skip went home. They were replaced by Al, a citizen of Panama who had been living in New York City when he was drafted. Larry had attended the University of Georgia, and Smitty had worked for IBM. Alan was the new battalion driver who helped out with typing when he was free.

How Al ended up in the army was not clear, even to him. He had thought he was reporting for a pre-induction physical and left the center in the army. Like me, he had been in the field with Alpha Company. He would go to Alpha's company clerk whenever he was back in camp and type for him. Larry was probably the best soldier of our group and had been in the field with Charlie Company. He was bigger and stronger than the rest of us, and would be competitive in any impromptu hairiest-chest contests. It was difficult to get him to talk about the war. I most identified with Smitty. Neither of us was convinced of the rightness or the wrongness of the war, and we both distrusted anyone who saw things unambiguously. He also had a better theory than I did on how decisions are made—why we get assigned where we get assigned, why missions are changed with no explanation, and why they keep making ham-and-lima C-rations. I figured it had to be a universe run by chance. They were random decisions by a bunch of computers somewhere in the basement of the Pentagon. The possible courses of action were all connected to random numbers selected by the computer. He corrected me. Decisions just aren't that rational. There were no computers, just an eighty-year-old woman in the basement of the Pentagon who makes every decision based on whatever she wants, usually her arthritis.

None of us had been trained as clerks. Each of our files listed infantry, 11B, as our Primary Military Occupational Specialty. We were all grunts, but now for ten hours a day, six days a week, and nine hours on the seventh, we filled out the paperwork for a combat battalion.

The company morning report is a daily status summary that provides information on the status of everyone in the company. Every change of status—transfers, leaves, AWOLs, KIAs,

MIAs—was entered in the company morning report. The company morning reports came to us right after the companies' morning formation. If someone transferred to another unit, the morning report reflected him as transferring out. His new unit would pick him up as transferring in the same day. If someone was missing or was wounded and in a hospital, that would be reflected in each unit's morning report.

Jim had done that, but when he left, it fell back to Sergeant Tom. He would check the entries to make sure everything that should be listed was listed properly, send it back to the company if it wasn't, and, when he had the completed set, send them to brigade.

There was a lot of routine typing. Each of us, as necessary, would type requests for orders, memoranda, and officer efficiency reports. Officer efficiency reports, or OERs, were the evaluations of performance that would make or break officers' careers. We all typed OERs when free. No more than two neatly corrected typing errors were allowed, or it had to be retyped. The end of a long day would often find one of us cussing at a typewriter that had just made its third mistake on its fifth or sixth try of an OER.

Officers were numerically rated by their supervisor against others who had served in that or a similar position. Like all evaluation forms, this one displayed "evaluation creep." Rating an officer below the eightieth percentile when compared to his peers was saying he had a limited future as an officer. There were specific questions, space for a narrative, and a recommendation for schooling ahead of or with his peers.

The most common problem was an inconsistency somewhere in the report. The most serious was with officers who insisted on "real" and accurate evaluations, who insisted the eightieth or some similar percentile was both an honest and a good evaluation, and who would hold onto that ranking even at the risk of damaging the career of the one they were evaluating. The content of the report was something we were to forget as soon as we typed it; it was none of our business. Although we could do nothing officially, we sometimes felt the need to say something unofficially.

The company commander who oversaw battalion supply and maintenance was an individual many of us had grown to admire. He had voluntarily helped us on details by finding the right piece of equipment or suggesting efficient ways to do things. Troops with specialties that keep them in the rear were perhaps more trouble-prone than others, and he was called on to administer punishments for those assigned to him. We had talked among ourselves about his response to a very tricky discipline problem. We believed him to genuinely care about those enlisted personnel he dealt with. He was also overweight and not particularly neat in appearance. I was in the office at night and could hear the executive officer yelling at him about his appearance, telling him to lose weight. His ratings on his military bearing doomed his career. I slipped out of the office so he wouldn't see me as he left battalion headquarters.

Several days later, he came through S-1, and I followed him as he left the building and caught up with him. I asked if I could say something and then told him we just wanted him to know how impressed we were with his way of dealing with the recent punishment he administered, that it served both S-4 and was in the best interest of the individual. "Anyway, sir, I was elected to tell you what we thought." I walked away quickly so that he would not have to respond.

The memoranda and awards and orders and efficiency reports were the routine. There were priorities in the office routine. Every morning, the casualty clerk would gather the figures on overnight casualties and then report the previous twenty-four hours' killed and wounded to the brigade S-1. As soon as someone was dusted off, the casualty clerk found out where the person was and what his medical status was. He would stay on the phone at night until he knew something.

Sergeant Tom called me to his desk one morning and told me I would be assigned casualties and morning reports. I would be exempted from guard duty and morning formations. Smitty took over awards and decorations.

Time would still not accelerate. Thanksgiving had been the first holiday that provided a temporal reference. It meant half a year had passed. A general flew in Thanksgiving morning, went only to the mess hall, inspected our paper turkey and paper pumpkin decorations, told the cooks that there had better be enough for everyone to have plenty, got back on his helicopter, and flew off for his next base, all in ten minutes.

CHAPTER 28

Life Goes On

I liked those with whom I shared Thanksgiving. We would have gotten along even without the common enemy we had in the company commander, who appeared to want us to understand he was in charge of our lives. We felt we could at least take care of our social relationships, but he was more than willing to intervene even there.

Performers came to the battalion every month or so, and one or two of us could attend. We took turns or, not remembering who attended last, drew straws. On the day of a show he had really wanted to see, Al believed he was entitled to go to the show because he had done so much work recently. He announced that he was going and was out the door. He probably had earned the right, but upset with his unilateral declaration, we had vowed retribution. We got the opportunity several weeks later. The adjutant said two of us needed to stay back; the rest could go to the show. I was not particularly interested in the show and so volunteered for one stay-behind slot. We then rigged the drawing so that Al stayed back. Unable simply to have put the universe back in moral order, someone bragged to one too many people of our deed, and word found its way to the company commander. He stormed into S-1, announcing that because we had cheated Al of an opportunity to go to the last show, he alone would go to the next one. The rest of us would work here or on detail. Nobody would speak. Nobody tried to explain why we had done what we had done. We did not know him well enough to know exactly what motivated him.

Those whose work kept them in the base camp—clerks and supply personnel and the motor pool mechanics—were not in the field. Most infantry soldiers would change places with them in an instant. But life in an isolated base camp was easy only by comparison to life in the field. It was a seven-day work week, the one concession being that we didn't have to get to work until 8:00 A.M. on Sundays. Almost the entire tour would be spent in an area perhaps 1,500 by 500 feet or moving from one such base camp to another. And even that estimate was generous since many never saw some areas of the base. Except for R and R and going home, life in the rear meant just that: life in the rear.

With my new responsibilities, I made a trip to brigade headquarters almost every day, delivering the battalion paperwork and picking up whatever was coming back to us. It also meant an occasional opportunity for a trip to the brigade PX. Usually, it was just the driver and I. We were vulnerable if anything happened. But I was not a prisoner of the base camp. Jim's reason for preferring Binh Phuoc to the division base camp at Dong Tam—its relative safety compared to the constant rocketing of Dong Tam—continued to hold after his departure. Every night, we would hear the mortars being fired into the district ARVN headquarters down the road. Fighting had been especially heavy the first four months of 1969. Occasionally, there would be intelligence probing of the base camp perimeter; small Viet Cong reconnaissance teams would check for anything vulnerable in our defenses. Inside the wire, we continued to be left alone. Maybe, I thought, it's a message: send troops home, and we won't bother those left behind. Or maybe they had moved out a comparable number of troops to some more active location now that they weren't here. It made as much sense as anyone's thoughts on the lack of activity in Long An Province.

At night, we would catch ourselves watching firefights in the distance. Green and red tracers raced toward each other. Red streams were drained from a Cobra's miniguns by the insatiable jungle below. Oblivious to my change in duties, time would still not accelerate.

I had a room that I shared with Larry, Al, and Smitty. The room was about eight by sixteen feet, with two bunk beds. We had mosquito netting over each bunk and were given one sheet that we could exchange once a week for a clean one. Nailed to our ceiling were sheets. We were located about twenty feet from the 4.2-inch mortar platoon. Our hootch shook every time they fired. The sheets on the ceiling caught the dirt and sawdust dislodged every time they fired their mortars. We had one desk for anyone who wanted to write, and previous occupants had built in a couple of small bookshelves that contained our "currently" and "get to next" books. Books were either those sent to the battalion by the Red Cross or those sent by family.

Inside the base camp, my entire life was within 100 feet of battalion headquarters. That was the distance from battalion headquarters to our sleeping quarters and from the back door of HQ to the mess hall. The company shower was twenty feet from our room, and the latrine was thirty feet in the other direction. Part way between battalion headquarters and our quarters was a movie screen for the nightly movie. Since I no longer visited the enlisted men's club, that 100-foot circle defined us.

If I hadn't been assigned the daily run to brigade headquarters, I would never have noticed how small my physical world had become.

Christmas made its appearance unaccompanied by Christmas spirit. A general appeared again to check the mess halls. The Christmas message to me was that I was past halfway in my year. But five months was still forever. Barely noticed, 1970 arrived.

Inside the camp the work routine was comfortable. I was good at my job. The daily reminders of war, the daily casualty report, and tracking down the prognosis for someone's wounds were my personal reminders. I knew I was off the line by luck, not merit. I became even more absorbed in my job, as if hard work would somehow change luck into merit. I assumed that I would continue doing what I was until I left Binh Phuoc in May.

That prospect didn't seem too bad. I liked my fellow clerks. I liked Sergeant Tom and Captain Bowes. The people in charge gave us as much responsibility as was reasonable. In return, we worked very hard.

CHAPTER 29

Another Kind of Courage

Mike was "Audie Murphy" to everyone in Alpha Company because of his bombastic patriotic proclamations from the top of the track at the end of a mission. He was my first thought when I found out why one of the officers from the tactical operations center, the TOC, wanted to talk to me. I had been in the TOC only two or three times despite its location only thirty feet down the hall from my desk. A map of the battalion operations area covered most of the visible space on one of its walls. Sometimes one, sometimes two radio telephone operators sat in front of the map. They kept the battalion in contact with each unit in the field and with the highers who would arrange air strikes if they were ever needed. At night, they also kept contact with every bunker on the base perimeter and with the sniper on the tower near the center of the base. If the base was ever attacked, my assigned position was outside the TOC.

The officer stopped at my desk. "Someone suggested I ask you. We would like to know if there is anyone you can recommend, someone currently in the field, someone we could bring into the TOC. We want a college graduate with some radio experience or who could learn quickly, and with enough time left in country so we won't have to retrain next month. We prefer someone who has been in a firefight. You know, someone who can be calm talking to guys in the field who are under fire and sound panicked. It has got to be someone who can keep up on several things happening at once."

I hesitated for a moment and told him Mike would be the best of those I knew.

149

"It may not work out," the captain said. "We've had some shake-and-bake sergeants who couldn't handle it."

I knew he was telling me that I needed to be absolutely honest.

"No helping out a friend. If he can't handle the pressure, find coordinates quickly, we'll send him back to his company. We don't want to have to do something like that."

"He can do it, sir."

Mike was assigned the job. He arranged to spend one more mission in the field with Alpha Company and then settled into the tactical operations center.

It turned out that the officers and senior NCOs in S-3 who worked in the TOC had a daily gambling pool. They each chose from the day's missions which one would make contact first. Each would put in a few dollars and pick from the day's projected missions.

When the story got to me, it was that Audie Murphy had refused to participate in some pool, standing up to the officers in the TOC. Word spread quickly about Audie Murphy refusing to play. When asked if he would like to get in on the pool, his reply according to the accounts spreading around the base was to the effect, "I've been there. I know those guys. I sure as hell am not going to get into a betting pool that amounts to making money on where somebody on your side is going to get shot at first."

I waited until it I could talk with him outside where no one might listen in. "You know you're a folk hero around the base, don't you?"

"I was afraid of that," he replied. "No big deal."

"You're not in trouble with anyone in S-3, are you?"

"No. If anything, it secured me. I just wasn't going to take part, and I let them know that. I owed turning it down to everyone out there. I think the pool is even still on. It's just not mentioned when I am around. Otherwise, I guess I'm just your run-of-the-mill folk hero."

We reached his barracks. "I never thought 'folk hero' was quite the right term," I explained. "You're really more of a Sunday School Lesson Hero."

"A what?"

"You're one of the heroes they taught us about on Sundays. Didn't want guys who were always getting in fights to be the poster boys for courage. They sought—and there were damn few of you—the kind of guy who would stand up to the crowd or who wouldn't let a group bully someone or who would not take off for the beach after school with a friend and a six pack. Anyway, that is how I'm billing you when I take you on tour after the war. We want those non-violent heroes who display real courage without getting into a fight. You're the guy from those stories."

"No six packs?"

"Maybe I went a little too far there. I was brought up a Baptist."

"One more thing," he said as he stepped back out of the doorway. "If I ever hear my name mentioned in conjunction with that phrase 'Sunday School Hero,' you might find that your DEROS has been moved up considerably. You better hope you Baptists have good hospitals." He headed for his bunk.

For a moment, I thought of a small sign hanging above his bed with "Home of the Sunday School Hero" printed on it. No, I thought, I should let him be a private hero; that would be better for him. And, frankly, I just wasn't too sure about those Baptist hospitals.

War doesn't have much use for the more psychological, less physical kinds of courage. Certainly, you would not want soldiers stopping to sort out and contemplate the issues they were dealing with. Maybe there aren't enough instances of it anyway, and besides, just how do you distinguish Bronze Star from Silver Star psychological heroism? And people know it when they see it. Audie, despite his protest, became a hero to a lot of soldiers.

CHAPTER 30

Failing Benny

I had finished checking the morning reports when Sergeant Tom cleared his throat, looked at me, and then rolled his head. I moved a chair beside him. He showed me a document and said it wasn't to leave his desk. I read the first sentence. I reread it. I had come across this policy once while reading regulations and ignored it. I hadn't put two and two together.

The premise was simple. Units might have unusually heavy influxes of personnel at times—for example, right after taking major losses in battle. At that point, you would have a larger-than-usual number of inexperienced soldiers in the unit and, consequently, a less effective unit. Further, this could become a recurring problem. Since large numbers came in at about the same time, they would be leaving at the same time. When they are replaced, the unit will once again have a larger number of inexperienced troops.

The military solution was to transfer soldiers with the ill-distributed DEROS date. If a unit appears to be facing a DEROS balloon payment, they should transfer a number of men with that DEROS date to other units and transfer in to replace them men with other DEROS dates. Any unit that would have more than some designated percentage scheduled to depart within a given period of time was subject to this reassignment policy.

Since two brigades of the 9th Division had gone home in August, anyone who was in those brigades who had been in country too little time to go home with his unit transferred into the remaining brigade. We were part of that brigade. We had taken in soldiers from departing units with March, April, and May arrival dates. In addition, we already had received our normal share of individuals through regular assignments during that time. Consequently, our brigade had approximately twice the number of soldiers with those departure dates than did typical units across Vietnam. To prevent us from losing too large a percentage of people—primarily with April, May, and June departures—a percentage of soldiers from our brigade with those dates would be reassigned across Vietnam. A comparable number from elsewhere and without the problematic DEROS dates would be assigned to us.

Militarily, there was a superficial logic to it. Too many replacements in a short period of time would mean less than the standard number of experienced soldiers. It ignored two facts, however. The policy assumes the way one fights is constant across the different terrains found in Vietnam. The army proposed that we take soldiers from those we were trying to help, taking their experience in the terrain they were familiar with against an enemy they were beginning to understand in a war where that really mattered. Everyone transferred out would probably know more than his replacement about how the war was best fought in his area.

It also ignored the personal effect. The policy promised devastating effects on the psyches of those being transferred, those who were fighting an already unpopular war with low morale. The support that sustained them, friendship forged in combat, was being taken away with little regard for the consequences. Soldiers with two or three or four months left would be uprooted to keep the statisticians happy. How likely were they to be as aggressive and risk-taking when needed?

These were not just abstract concerns. I was in that arrival pool. I had arrived in May. My primary MOS, military occupational specialty, was still 11B, infantry. Not only could I be transferred, but I would be transferred as an infantryman. I could finish my tour back in the field, in a new terrain. I would have to start all over again.

I quickly reviewed the regulations and then asked Sergeant Tom if I could talk to him. I noted that he stood to lose all but one of the enlisted personnel in S-1. I told him the battalion could request a limited number of waivers, exempting anyone considered key personnel. He jotted down some notes and walked into the adjutant's office. Moments later, they walked in to see the executive officer together.

I wasn't sure what S-1 would do. I hoped someone would argue that some of us would be hard to replace. Two days passed. We heard nothing. We speculated on where we would be sent. Most logical, it seemed, were places that had sustained heavy casualties recently. Reluctantly, I dropped the second shoe. We all had an infantry MOS. We would be going to units that would already have a staffed S-1 or company headquarters. It would be too much to ask that a clerical job that became available go to someone who was transferring into the unit. Your six or seven or eight months in the field would not equal six or seven or eight months for the home team. We tried to continue working, but work was constantly interrupted by some newfound reason to worry. We waited, death-row prisoners waiting for the governor's call.

Sergeant Tom delivered the reprieve on day three of our wait. A waiver had been requested for everyone in S-1. Most likely, nobody would be transferring.

"Nothing certain yet. Looks good. But be ready for bad news, just in case."

A day after hearing that waivers had been requested, I was told there was someone in front of battalion headquarters who wanted to see me but did not want to come in. Benny was the squad's machine gunner when I first arrived in Alpha Company. It was Benny I sat with in a water-filled crater in the Plain of Reeds expecting to be shot by our own helicopter.

He showed me orders transferring him to another mechanized infantry unit and asked what was going on. I had been so focused on myself that I hadn't thought of the squad or those I knew who would be affected. But I also did not have any idea of where to start trying to help him.

I explained the policy to him and then told him his best bet was to go to the current Two Six and try for a waiver. "You have got to be close to senior in the platoon," I noted.

"Nobody you can go to?" he asked.

"I'll try, but it's probably best to start with Two Six. If you want, I'll talk to him."

"You being transferred?" he asked, his frustration starting to show.

I told him that a waiver had been requested and that I'd have to wait to know. I mentioned the possibility that, given how little time he had left in country, he might get sent to the rear if transferred. I urged him to talk to someone in his chain of command about a waiver.

"Can you do anything?" he repeated.

"I'll try."

He left angry. He was counting on me to be able to do something. It certainly looked like I had gotten the breaks. With less time in country, I got off the line first. Now I might be spared assignment elsewhere. He was right. I had gotten the breaks

I got on the phone with Benny's company clerk, asking if anything could be done. He said he didn't think so, and when I asked if he would talk to the captain to make sure he knew about the waivers, he very sharply told me it was none of my business and hung up.

I went to Sergeant Tom.

"He was right. It was none of your business. If his CO is not doing anything, nothing you can do," Sergeant Tom told me.

For the second time, those on the line were ripped away from, or had ripped away from them, the one thing in this war that meant something to them. Benny's friends had gone home while he stayed in August and September. Now he was being sent away from any new friendships he had secured to start over again with three months to go. I felt sick. I had left Benny behind a second time. I didn't know what was worse, my inability to help him or the fact he thought that I could but hadn't. Several weeks later, I got a terse, one-sentence report from someone Benny had asked to deliver to me: "He said to tell you he's not in the rear, but on the line fighting in the jungle."

Benny, the warrior, was not essential personnel in war. I was a clerk. I was.

CHAPTER 31

Time Out

In the rear, it was a seven-days-a-week job. We escaped the routine a few minutes or a few hours at a time.

Armed Forces Vietnam provided popular music—anything from country "I know you're cheatin' on me" songs to Frank Sinatra ballads to top forty rock and roll. In our hootch at night, or barely audible in the office during the day, it was the background of our lives. Al was a Frank Sinatra fan, and he could not mention Sinatra without connecting him to a song title or fragment of lyric. It was always "Frank Sinatra, he did it his way" or "Frank Sinatra, life's been good to him."

Many of us had a "home song," the song that had come to embody all the emotions about going home. For the country troops, it was "Green, Green Grass of Home." For me, as it was for many, it was Mary Travers singing "Leaving on a Jet Plane." That one line expressed the hope that we would not let go of. The home songs were all more than songs.

At night, if we didn't watch a movie, we would write letters home. Al would strum the guitar and sing. Almost every night, we would hear "La Bamba," with Al stopping to explain nuances of the lyrics: "I am not a sailor. I am the captain." And we talked. About our lives before Vietnam. About our families. That all seemed so distant, as if the images were pictures from a book written long, long ago.

From time to time, live entertainment would be brought to the base, most often a Korean band accompanied by go-go dancers and with a lead singer who would phonetically mispronounce the words of the songs she sang. They all did a rendition of The Animals' "We've Gotta Get Out of This Place." It was an anthem. We would sing along, changing "work" to "short" in the refrain. More than entertainment, the shows also provided a window on race relations in the U.S. Army.

Smitty and I had won the drawing and were off for a couple of hours for this afternoon's show. We were sitting by members of the scout platoon, learning the details of a recent mission that was the talk of the battalion. They described the helicopter assault where they dropped in at night on the wedding of the daughter of a Viet Cong official. Even during war, you listen to good war stories.

The story was interrupted by the band, which kicked off with early Beatles, followed by something soul and then something country. Something for everyone. As the third or fourth song ended, Smitty tapped me on the shoulder and pointed to a section of the crowd. Applause, it appeared, was being meted out along some racial criterion. Black soldiers were applauding only soul songs, the country contingent only country songs. Each greeted the other's songs with stone-faced indifference. The army, which prided itself on being ahead of the curve on race relations, was a reflection of the world around it.

Smitty and I had been applauding everything. We also considered ourselves centrally located rock-and-roll fans. We had grown up on AM top forty rock and roll. Smitty laughed at the conjunction of musical taste and our tolerance across musical types.

"Guess it's true," he observed. "If it's going to get done, it's going have to be rock and roll that will save the world."

"Roger that. Love is all you need."

Ignoring the crowd's reactions, I let the music take me away from the war. I spent the next hour back in the world, driving up and down the anointed avenue with the David and Walt and a blasting radio, at a fraternity party, and parked in a dorm parking lot on a Friday night as the approaching curfew raced with fumbling desire. Smitty, I suspected, was also a long way from Southeast Asia.

The army made an elaborate production of Thanksgiving and Christmas, with a general flying in for each to check mess hall preparations. I had to admit the army did holidays pretty well. We wanted to help everyone celebrate a different holiday, one the army forgot. Making the sign and hiding it in our hootch was the easy part. We still needed to get off the base. That task was turned over to the battalion drivers who checked out the jeeps for routine maintenance. We counted on having either the colonel's jeep or the major's and on nobody challenging either of them.

"Why all the whispered talk?" Sergeant Tom asked.

"Nothing," we assured him. "Just trying not to disturb anyone."

We got back to our routine, aware that even talking to each other was not wise. The driver lipped back into the office, smiling. We waited. A couple of hours passed. Nothing. And then a series of whispered conversations around us.

"What's up?" Smitty asked Sergeant Tom.

"Seems there's a sign on Thunder Road—'McDonald's: Next Right.' Even got the arches on it. Nobody in here would know anything about that, I hope." Sergeant Tom waited to see one of us respond. Nobody confessed. "Nobody knows anything. Good. Nobody better learn anything either. That is an order."

We carried on feigned conversations about how it might have happened and who might have been responsible, but Sergeant Tom's look backed us off.

Smitty and I set out for lunch. "You suppose the VC know about April Fools' Day?"

Smitty thought a moment. "Some VC intelligence officer is probably meeting with his CO right now, trying to make sense of the arches."

R and R was the real trip away from the war. A week in a place where there was no war. A week to recharge. The army flew you there. Everything else was paid for by you. There were several choices. Tokyo was the destination of those interested in electronics. Hawaii was the place for married soldiers whose spouses would be flown there to meet them. Thailand was there for those who sought only sex, and Australia was the choice of those who naively thought they would be going to a country where the population spoke the same language they did. Al had already gone on R and R, having flown to Hawaii to become a United States citizen.

I had always assumed I would probably just skip R and R, but after my encounter with Benny, I felt for the first time I really wanted to get away for a few days. Sergeant Tom told me to be sure to come back. He was getting along quite well without morning reports piled on his desk every morning. I put in my request, not expecting to get a slot for a while. A couple of weeks later, I was in the R and R center near Saigon, taking my first hot shower since arriving in country, spending my first night between two sheets. For the first time since last May, I felt clean.

The flight to Sydney took eight hours. Eight hours from the war. Eight more hours for the war to somehow end. Our landing was delayed as we waited for morning. Airlines faced large fines if they flew low or landed before dawn. At the R and R center, we could purchase or rent civilian clothes. I rented. After an hour's delay at immigration because the base doctor in Binh Phuoc had stamped rather than signed my health card when he certified me free of any venereal disease, I was delivered to a hotel.

At the hotel, I watched ten minutes of television. It hadn't changed. I went outside and just walked the streets, staring into store windows. I had walked for less than a half an hour when I was stopped by a woman who ran one of the many dating services. I followed her into her office. Her business was to direct soldiers and their dates to selected clubs and restaurants by means of discount coupons. They supplied the dates.

The woman who had spotted me as a soldier on R and R asked what I was looking for in a date. I told her I hadn't had a conversation with anyone but other soldiers for a long time, and I wanted someone who would be fun to talk to, and moral relativism, while okay, was not a deal-breaker. They told me they had just the person, a nurse who was taking a few months' leave from work.

We met that night. At our first stop, a bar for which I had two discount tickets, she suggested dinner at a place not on the list, a restaurant built from a 150-year-old house. They knew her by name when we arrived. We talked. We also danced. We stayed on the floor when a fast song forced the others to their seats. We were acknowledged with a round of applause, more likely a statement of Australian political support for the war than a recognition of any talent on my part.

After dinner, and after several more drinks, she mentioned having new friends who were part of the lesbian community in Sydney and suggested we go visit a bar where they hung out. I picked up the dessert menu and suggested something chocolate instead.

One day that week, I went to the movies and saw *The Prime of Miss Jean Brodie,* another story whose background was a war without a side that deserved to win.

A week after departing Binh Phuoc, I was back. Twenty minutes into my morning, the sergeant major told me to use my lunch hour to trim my mustache and get a haircut. Eight hours was not far enough.

CHAPTER 32

Prisoners of War

Outside the wire, the war continued. A defector walked out of the jungle, surrendered, and then on a flyover pointed out the location of what turned out to be an enemy field hospital. Among those captured was a woman doctor, thought to be NVA. The prisoners were being held overnight twenty feet down the hall in S-2, the intelligence section, until they could be interrogated.

The morning after the raid, as I usually did, I came to S-1 early to get a start on the day's work while the office was quiet. Before I understood what had happened, the sergeant who had been up all night watching the prisoners turned them over to me to watch while he ate and showered. I protested I was a clerk and not qualified to watch prisoners. He noted they were handcuffed and assured me someone would soon be here to take over in a few minutes and he would be back as quickly as he could eat and shower. Ignoring my protest, he left. Suddenly, they were my prisoners.

I went to look at my prisoners. They looked scared. Assuming they wouldn't understand my words, I tried to convey something by speaking softly. "Don't worry," I said, trying to sound comforting. "You are prisoners of S-1. The most we will do is mess up your paperwork." Most just continued looking down. The woman stared at me defiantly. Maybe she was a true believer. Maybe she was upset by what had been reported as a very enthusiastic body search when she was captured. When the mess hall opened, I stopped someone walking by the office door and asked him to bring back several plates of scrambled eggs, which I distributed to the detainees. The woman refused to eat. She glared at me, her eyes revealing the hatred and

161

contempt she carried. I shrugged my shoulders, marched away loudly, and then turned and sneaked back up the hall. I stared over the opening and watched her eat. Then, after a minute, she looked up.

"Gotcha." I smiled. She looked away, obviously embarrassed. I issued an apology that wouldn't be understood, but seemed called for, and took a seat in S-1 where I could see anyone moving or hear anyone talking.

The intelligence team arrived a half hour later. They were furious, the officer in charge demanding to know by whose authority I had fed their prisoners. The Third Geneva Conventions turned out not to be the answer he was looking for.

What I didn't think about, I was told, was that I might have prevented the interrogation team from getting valuable information, that my actions might be responsible for future American deaths.

"Just a minute," I interrupted. "Let's go talk to somebody. In fact, let's go talk to whoever you want to talk to about this. I want to make sure he knows that the person you left in charge of the prisoners just walked off and turned them over to me without instructions and over my protest. In fact, he didn't even ask if I would. Said he needed breakfast and would be right back. That's almost an hour ago, and he is still not here."

His tone changed. He did not want to battle over it. "It's important to keep them disoriented before you interrogate them," he explained.

"I'm pretty sure I helped on that score," I said.

CHAPTER 33

Making Sergeant

I told myself that if I made sergeant, there would be no KP for the seven months of stateside duty I would have left after returning from Vietnam. The real reasons had more to do with ego than with washing dishes. I thought I had earned it. I knew I wasn't doing the most important work or the hardest work of the war. I knew that belonged to those in the field. But I also believed that I worked long and hard and that what I was doing I did very well. I wanted to know that my efforts had been recognized. And buried at some distance within me, I wanted the prestige.

For promotion to sergeant, there was a promotion board made of senior noncommissioned officers. Their recommendation would be based on performance record, military bearing during the interview, knowledge of one's job, and knowledge of current events. Only the last one seemed anything I could prepare for. We all got our knowledge of current events from the same place, the military's newspaper, *Stars and Stripes*. I secured all the back copies I could and read and reread them. I felt pretty confident that I would have something to say about any current events questions I got. All that time in school studying for tests had prepared me well for one thing: studying for tests.

The day arrived. I was called in from the waiting room, which turned out to be the S-1, walked into what turned out to be the intelligence interrogation room, and stood next to a chair obviously meant for me until I was asked to sit down. The current events question was about Jane Fonda. Why had she been in the news recently? What was she up to now?

I noted her involvement in an American Indian protest, mentioning the general issues. One of the members of the board added some detail to my answer. I acknowledged his better answer. Senior NCOs are a mixed group, sometimes terribly bright individuals who feel they see to the day-to-day work getting done, but that their ability is not appreciated. A second unscripted question came from the promotion board. What did I think of Jane Fonda? There was a little quick chatter among the board members about whether they could ask that and told me I didn't need to answer.

There were questions about my record and about my time in the field about what a typical day was like. The technical questions on things a sergeant should know were questions I could answer quickly and concisely. The last question was the one I heard about from the person who interviewed immediately before me. I had been called in before I had time to think about answering it. "You're an infantry MOS, Specialist Carr," the question began. "Since infantry is your primary specialty, suppose that getting the promotion meant rejoining an infantry company. What if going into the field and serving in your MOS was a condition of getting promoted to sergeant?"

I turned to the sergeant who had added to my Jane Fonda answer. "I don't suppose you'd like to take this one for me, sergeant?" I asked.

Everyone laughed except one first sergeant. I thought for a few seconds. The question they were asking meant choosing between the promotion and the rear. I answered a different question.

"I think I'm doing a good job at what I do, and quite frankly, I'm not sure how effective I would be right now out in the field. But I believe that everyone in this room would do what he was asked to do, go where he was asked to go. If promoted. If not promoted." I knew from the nodding heads I had put the question away. I hoped nobody would ask in their discussion precisely what my answer to their last question had been.

"Thank you, specialist. Do you have any questions?"

I indicated that I did not.

"Tell the next person waiting we will call him when we are ready."

"Yes, first sergeant." I stepped to the side as I got out of my chair so I could do a sharp 180.

When the promotion list came out, I was number two in the battalion. Ahead of me was someone who had also interviewed the day I got the job in S-1. He had gotten the other job and had been a radio telephone operator with the district ARVN unit, I was told. He had recently returned to the battalion and was working in the tactical operations center.

"Fair enough," I thought. Regardless of how his interview went, I knew that I would have put him number one on my list.

The next set of orders approved two from the battalion for promotion.

CHAPTER 34

War

The Chinese Claymore is larger than ours, but the basic idea is the same. Fragments of metal are accelerated by plastic explosive packed behind them, tearing apart everything in front of the kill zone. We usually encountered them hanging in the trees. They could either be set up to explode when someone stepped on a trip wire or detonated by someone hidden within fifty feet of it.

I was sitting at my desk when a runner from the tactical operations center delivered the message: "Casualties." At least one was killed in action, and among the wounded was the platoon leader, a lieutenant. I passed my current work to someone else and called the brigade aid station, usually the first stop for those dusted off. They reported the flight had gone directly to the surgical hospital at Long Binh, an indication the wounds were serious. I reported that to Sergeant Tom, who took the information on up the chain of command.

I then began the process of working from switchboard to switchboard to switchboard until I connected with the one serving Long Binh. I would pick up the telephone and get our battalion switchboard. I would ask for the Tan An switchboard and would be connected to it. I would ask the operator at that switchboard to connect me with another switchboard until I was connected to one that could connect me with the hospital. In the meantime Vietnamese operators at all those intermediate switchboards wanted to recapture their line. They would inquire, "Working?" If the reply—"Working!"—wasn't given loudly or quickly enough, the operator would disconnect the call, and the process would start over at the battalion switchboard.

After several restarts, I got hold of the brigade liaison at the surgical hospital who gave me the report. I reported the lieutenant's critical condition to S-1, who had asked to be notified as soon as I got any new information. While I was on the phone, some information about the cause of the injuries became available. A Claymore mine hanging in a tree was detonated. The Vietnamese Tiger Scout who worked with the platoon was killed instantly. The platoon leader was the most serious of the wounded.

For several days, his condition had remained critical. I had been calling the hospital each morning and then coming back after dinner to see if there had been any change during the day. I took a shower after dinner, walked back to the office.

I got through, identified myself, and asked for the liaison. A short note was waiting for me: "Died of wounds." I stepped out of the back door of S-1 and crossed the few feet to the door of the officers' club. I stood in the doorway until I caught someone's attention and asked to see the adjutant. I told him and went back to my desk.

The families of those killed received a letter from the soldier's commanding officer. The army had a form letter with places to add specific material. The family would know what kind of operation, just what the cause of death was, and a location that could be looked up on a map that showed provinces. In case those killed had both a spouse and parents, the army had two slightly different versions. It gave the letters a more individual appearance. The lieutenant was leaving behind a wife and children as well as parents. I typed two letters, one to his wife and one to his parents, inserting slightly different descriptions in each. I put them in the S-1's box the next morning.

When he came in, the company commander thanked me for the letters but said he had an obligation to write the letters himself.

When an enlisted man below the rank of specialist was killed in action, the individual could be posthumously promoted one rank and given a posthumous medal. It had become so routine that I did not remember it not being done. It was seen as a way of trying to acknowledge the individual's sacrifice.

The private in this case was an American Indian, friendly and good natured, but neither a good nor dedicated soldier. He was assigned to Headquarters Company and worked in the rear. The company commander did not like him and regarded his attitude and actions as borderline insubordination. He was ordered out on a mission with the scout platoon, primarily as a means of trying to motivate him. Early the next morning, I got the report.

Last night, the Scouts had called for illumination. The flares lit and slowly floated downward. The now useless canisters fell toward the earth, accelerating downward at thirty-two feet per second per second. In a freakish accident of friendly fire, one canister fell, hit, and killed a Native American soldier.

The company commander refused to recommend the soldier for posthumous promotion, informing the S-1, "He was a terrible soldier, and it would be an insult to those who had died carrying out their duty to promote him."

It was his call, but that did not prevent a debate in the company. Those who defended the decision echoed the CO's argument. It would demean the sacrifice of those who had performed more honorably. It would not be meaningful in the future.

The critics argued that he was on a mission doing what he had been asked to do, that doing your duty didn't require doing it enthusiastically, or even that you do it well. The captain's defenders countered that promotion was based on long-term performance, and he did not merit it. The critic's counter to the counter was that this meant those killed shortly after arrival could not be promoted.

The company commander, in the office to see the adjutant, was aware of the debate in his company. As he left the office, he stopped by my desk. "You're one of those who thinks I'm wrong, aren't you, Carr?"

"Sir, I'm one of those glad he's not making the decision." I had offered an olive branch.

He just kept walking.

We want it to make sense. But war kills without regard to merit, without regard to character. The families it touches are all equally devastated. Each of its victims is robbed of the rest of his future. And it leaves with those who survive the knowledge that in large measure they survived because they were lucky. Lucky! Who do you owe for that? How do you pay the debt? How do you ever make that right?

CHAPTER 35

Leaving Binh Phuoc

The year was passing, a passing that did not answer the questions it asked. Neither side walked with the angels. The South was corrupt. Everything was for sale, including my socks. It was a society of wealth and privilege. The North was brutally totalitarian. Life mattered little to its leaders. It was there to be used in the pursuit of social goals. If I were asked who I would prefer to see win, it would be the South. But why was helping the lesser of two evils worth a million lives?

Defenders and critics of the war each told a partial story. Critics of the war ignored the brutal, oppressive character of the North. On the other hand, those who said stopping the North was a just action never explained why that would entitle our government to force its citizens to go risk their lives in service of that cause.

Of two undeserving sides, we chose to fight alongside those who would not fight. They might have been right in making that judgment. That should not have been without effect on our policymakers.

The country that sent us to fight that war was divided in its assessment of the worth of fighting it. You fought, knowing more than half of the population back home did not support what you were doing. We were told to go risk death for something most of our fellow citizens believed wrong.

Was there a real difference in the way it was fought? A strategy that sent soldiers into the field with those in charge hoping that they would be hit so we could hit back harder was not very far from a policy of sacrificing our lives for no purpose other than taking more of theirs. What stayed out of the focus of any moral lens was whether this was true of all wars or just this war.

Did the fact that our intent was to trade lives at a favorable enough ratio cash out differently than another war's intent to take a piece of real estate and give up lives for it? Were this war's managers more cynical or simply more honest about what war finally is?

And then there was the policy that sent Benny and thousands of others out, for the second or third time, to be the new guy who would once again be called on to fight a war unpopular at home, a war where you had no reason to believe that your country valued your sacrifice, all without the presence of those whose trust and respect you had earned, whose presence was what made facing each day possible. Did those calculating combat effectiveness stop for a moment to figure the emotional cost for the soldier who, with no explanation or warning, was handed orders one morning that would rip him away from all he really had? Didn't they realize that those transferring in with four or five months left were going to be suspect by their new unit?

Even in the midst of this uncertainty, I had met and lived with and written for those who, whatever their own views, were here because this is what they believed their fellow citizens expected of them and who, though they wanted desperately to survive for one year, were willing to risk their lives for their comrades when the moment demanded, knowing they were bait in a body-count war.

But there was one last piece of the master's puzzle. What brought all of this together was "the year." As the war dragged on, it became the overarching goal: last one year. That's what you're here for. Nothing else offered to you meant anything. The war was about surviving your year. But it is a year whose length does not diminish as May becomes June, June becomes July. The time doesn't move on. It is always your year. There is no "feel" to being nine months out that is any different from the feel of being eight months out. It continues not to move until, one day, you are told it is over and you are going home. That's what you could not tell the new guy, that he was here for a year, and no matter even if you had survived some of it, there was still the forever-year of nine months or seven months to go. His year was about lasting his endless year that suddenly was passing with a day or a week or two weeks left. It was there in the PFC's warning when I first found I was going to Dong Tam, "Watch out for Charles. Charles will DEROS you."

My year would be over. Moments that had displayed the ability to extend their duration felt suddenly on the verge of compressing. I found myself fighting the temptation to start counting the days—if only because that's what you did at a certain point. But whatever level of safety and comfort I had come to feel, I had never considered extending my tour in Vietnam for an early release from the army.

Things change with small events, often the warnings of change. Normally friendly troops from the classified communications cage appear to want to talk, but cannot. A battalion commander is pulled from a mission and becomes preoccupied with maps in his office late at night. Those who were heard speculating about what might be up were warned of the dangers of rumors to morale. Clearly, something was up. A communication specialist unable to contain it any longer walked through S-1 one night and whispered, "It's Cambodia."

Out of the hearing of officers or senior NCOs, the speculation continued. "He may be guessing too," Smitty said. The worst-case scenario was we were going to invade Cambodia.

To everyone's relief, the orders that came down did not mention Cambodia. In a week, the battalion would be leaving Binh Phuoc permanently. Headquarters elements would move to Bear Cat, the original home of the 9th Division, twenty-five miles east of Saigon. The battalion would become mobile, staying in the field. The battalion from Rach Kien would move to Binh Phuoc. In fact, they had already started some missions in our area of operations and quickly embarrassed us by finding an underground enemy complex that had been here for years.

There was more. Everyone in the battalion whose DEROS date was in May would be going home early. My tour in Vietnam would be eleven months. The explanation we got was that they didn't want the complications of people going home while the bugs were worked out in the new administrative and operational procedures involved in forming an entirely mobile battalion. I reached a different conclusion. It was a different complication they were trying to avoid. Those who speculated we were going to Cambodia had to be right. They did not want the extra complication of DEROS dates during what was going to be one large operation. I could not make sense of any alternative.

The days became a confusion of packing and loading, of liberating trailers from other areas of the camp only to have them stolen. The pace was so swift that I didn't have time to think about the fact I would be going home. I was excited but didn't have time to feel what I knew I should be feeling.

I had assumed I would be going to Bear Cat for a few days, but Captain Bowes told me that I was too short and that he had arranged for me to go to brigade headquarters in Tan An for a week as liaison with brigade S-1 during the transition. I got a day and a half's notice. The rest of those with May departure dates would stay and work in Binh Phuoc until they got their orders to leave. I barely had time to say good-bye to Al and Smitty, who would be going to Bear Cat. The night before leaving, I sang "La Bamba" one last time with Al, explaining the nuances of the Spanish. Satisfied that I understood the song, he told me it was okay to leave. I spent my last night in Binh Phuoc.

Eleven months earlier, I had arrived in Binh Phuoc in the battalion mail truck. My last day, I threw my duffel bag in the back of the same mail truck and waited with the driver for the other passenger. As we waited, Armed Forces Radio played "Leaving on a Jet Plane." I couldn't have framed the eleven months any better. Forty-five minutes later, the driver delivered me to brigade headquarters in Tan An.

There was little for me to do in Tan An. The clerks in brigade S-1 declined my offer of any help they could use, saying I had earned a few days off. I spent a few hours with someone who agreed to show me how to develop film, but I was unable to pay attention. With nothing to do, my final days inched forward.

The first night in Tan An, a twenty-foot-tall Jacqueline Bis-set emerged topless from the ocean to the cheers of several dozen soldiers. By the time movies reached Binh Phuoc, most nude scenes had been snipped off, added to someone's private collection.

The next day, there were two arrivals from Binh Phuoc, the first of those with May arrival dates, I assumed. I knew one of them well. I asked if the move had gotten off on the right foot.

"Almost," one explained. "You remember the battalion commander gave orders that units were not to bring their dogs with them, that they would hinder operations in the field?"

I nodded.

"You know the colonel has his dog, Jo Jo. Turns out there was lots of mysterious radio traffic with oblique references to 'Juliet Juliet.' They get to night-laager position, they let down the ramp on the colonel's track, and out runs Jo Jo. After telling everyone to leave their dogs at Binh Phuoc, he brings his. The colonel brought his dog. Then other tracks drop their ramps to set up for the night, and maybe a dozen or more dogs start running around."

"Anyway," said the second, "we heard you were here work-ing at brigade, and we need to talk to you."

"What's up?"

He described what he claimed were the conditions for the 2/47 troops left at Binh Phuoc. They worked ten to twelve hours a day but weren't allowed to eat in the mess hall. Instead, they were given C-rations.

"They have us work all day for them, putting up new bar-racks and rearranging old ones. Then, since we don't go out in the field with their units, they say we can't eat in their mess halls. We live on Cs. Someone talked to the MPs earlier, and we wanted to follow up with you."

"We'll take care of them," I promised.

I didn't know who to tell, but I couldn't stand by and do nothing. I did not know how to help Benny when he needed my help. Not knowing whom to go to, I went to my counterpart at brigade S-1 and told a clerk. He said he would pass the information on. Within minutes, a lieutenant emerged and started asking them questions. They started retelling the story. I nodded, slipped out the door, and walked to the main gate to talk to one of the MPs at the gate. An officer there interrupted me. A truck would bring the rest of them to Tan An, where they would stay until their departure dates. The MPs had probably taken care of the matter before I began my intervention. But maybe, just maybe, I had done some good for my comrades.

It was my last act for the 2/47.

CHAPTER 36

Going Home

April 22, 1970. I walked to the flight line at the Tan An airfield and caught a flight to Long Binh, where I had processed in country almost twelve months before. Faces familiar from Fort Lewis, faces I had not seen in a year, were scattered across the company area. They too were getting out early, more evidence for me of the size of the coming operation. Some had news of those who did not make it, including the person who bunked next to me in infantry training at Fort Lewis, a Hispanic soldier with a great imitation of our drill sergeant.

This time, Long Binh held no work details for us. We were told to show up for formations. The formations were the exit from Vietnam. We needed no encouragement.

To be here, to be going home, had been the one constant motivation in my life, and probably in the lives of all those around me, for most of a year, but whatever emotions I had expected to accompany the moment appeared AWOL. Any way I tried to feel felt like an act. I was numb, as if all emotion had long ago been used up.

Another formation. Then another. And finally, "Carr, Charles. Sergeant."

"Here, sir!" I answered, and then as I had done so many times, I followed the man in front of me.

At Binh Hoa airport, we endured one last inspection of our duffel bags to make sure we were not carrying part of Vietnam home with us. With 200 others, I settled into bleachers shaded from the sun just off the flight lines. Worn, faded, salt-stained jungle fatigues identified us to each other. Some carried on occasional conversations, but most simply waited, watching planes take off and land in the distance. The screams of jets taking off on bombing missions were our reminder that the war continued without us.

Planes taxied toward us and then turned off. Finally, one didn't. A few stood to watch it. Then a few more. The plane taxied toward us, interrupting now forced conversations. Every head turned in its direction. Soon everyone was standing. Applause and cheers moved across the bleachers as weary soldiers began to acknowledge the moment. The cheering continued as the plane emptied itself of kids with new fatigues and frightened faces. It continued as they turned to march past us. Decibel by decibel, the noise stretched upward. Expressing what we couldn't, it would not be stopped. The uncomprehending soldiers stared back at us as they moved past, a year from being able to understand their first moments.

The wheel had turned one circle. But it was our turn of the circle. Others were now where we had been a year ago. We were now where others had been when we took our first hesitant steps. We felt now what they felt, understood what they understood. Like them, we had somehow found our way to this moment. We were here.

I was here. I had survived. No other thought, no other image, could find room in this moment. There would be a lifetime to think about those loved and about those left behind. A lifetime to remember moments of terror and moments of joy, to remember a February new guy I had never met. A lifetime to try to make sense of the randomness that brought me to this moment and left on the battlefield those so much better. A lifetime to try to find peace. But this moment, this joy, was only about now. My year is over. I am going home.

Epilogue

Some believe there is one story that is the story of all stories. One version of it tells us that the stuff of the universe is space-time. It asks that we not think of events as past or future. Rather, think of those events as spread timelessly at some location on the fabric of spacetime. Past events have not vanished. They are where they have always been, at their location, at their address, in space-time. We are now at all those addresses that have or will ever include us. We *are* at every place we ever were or will be.

Strange to find comfort in physics, but it seems somehow reassuring. Our past moments have not vanished. In some timeless eternal now, frightened kids are returning from a mission and beginning one and writing home and arguing about what day it is and making fun of a squad leader teaching himself the harmonica and getting ready to assault a wood line. And at all those moments, in ways only they understand, they depend on and care for and love each other.

Stackpole Military History Series

Real battles. Real soldiers. Real stories.

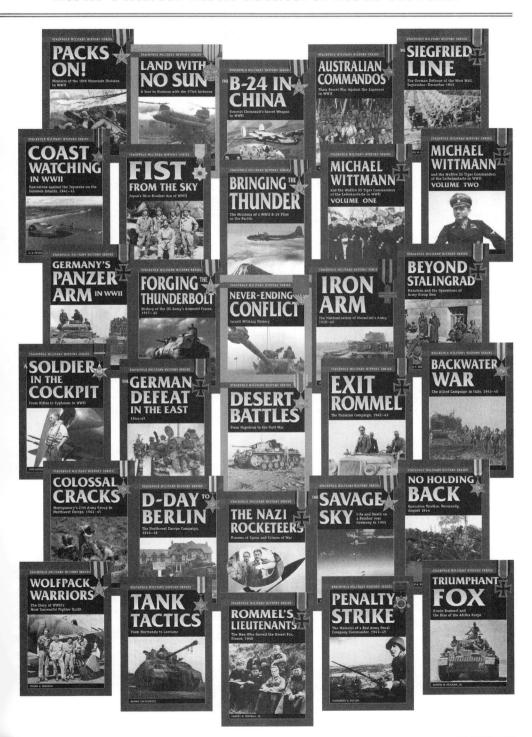

Stackpole Military History Series

Real battles. Real soldiers. Real stories.

Real battles. Real soldiers. Real stories.

STACKPOLE MILITARY HISTORY SERIES

TWO ONE PONY
An American Soldier's Year in Vietnam, 1969

STACKPOLE MILITARY HISTORY SERIES

JAPANESE ARMY FIGHTER ACES
1931–45

NEW for Spring 2012

STACKPOLE MILITARY HISTORY SERIES

JG 26 LUFTWAFFE FIGHTER SQUADRON WAR DIARY
Volume One: 1939–42

DONALD CAL

STACKPOLE MILITARY HISTORY SERIES

PANZER WEDGE
The 3rd Panzer Division's Drive on Moscow, 1941

STACKPOLE MILITARY HISTORY SERIES

THE SPARTAN ARMY
J.F. LAZENBY

STACKPOLE MILITARY HISTORY SERIES

WAR OF THE WHITE DEATH
Finland against the Soviet Union, 1939–40

BAIR IRINCHEEV

STACKPOLE MILITARY HISTORY SERIES

WINTER STORM
The Battle for Stalingrad and the Operation to Rescue 6th Army

HANS WIJERS

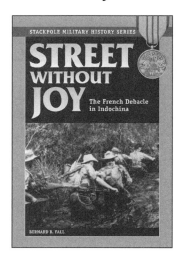

Stackpole Military History Series

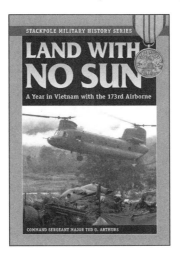

LAND WITH NO SUN

A YEAR IN VIETNAM WITH THE 173RD AIRBORNE

Command Sergeant Major Ted G. Arthurs

You know it's going to be hot when your brigade is referred to as a fireball unit. From May 1967 through May 1968, the Sky Soldiers of the 173rd Airborne were in the thick of it, humping eighty-pound rucksacks through triple-canopy jungle and chasing down the Viet Cong and North Vietnamese in the Central Highlands of South Vietnam. As sergeant major for a battalion of 800 men, it was Ted Arthurs's job to see them through this jungle hell and get them back home again.

$21.95 • Paperback • 6 x 9 • 416 pages • 60 b/w photos

Stackpole Military History Series

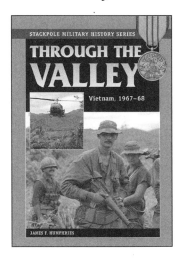

THROUGH THE VALLEY

VIETNAM, 1967–68

Col. James F. Humphries

In the remote northern provinces of South Vietnam—
a region of long-forgotten villages and steep hills—
the U.S. Americal Division and 196th Light Infantry
Brigade fought a series of battles against the North
Vietnamese and Vietcong in 1967–68: Hiep Duc, Nhi Ha,
Hill 406, and others. These pitched engagements, marked
by fierce close combat, have gone virtually unreported in
the decades since, but Col. James F. Humphries brings
them into sharp focus, chronicling the efforts of these
proud American units against a stubborn enemy and
reconstructing what it was like to fight in Vietnam.

$19.95 • Paperback • 6 x 9 • 384 pages • 47 b/w photos, 24 maps

WWW.STACKPOLEBOOKS.COM
1-800-732-3669

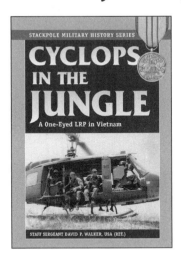

Stackpole Military History Series

EXPENDABLE WARRIORS
THE BATTLE OF KHE SANH AND THE VIETNAM WAR
Bruce B. G. Clarke

On January 21, 1968, nine days before the Tet Offensive, thousands of North Vietnamese soldiers attacked the U.S. Marine base at Khe Sanh in remote northwestern South Vietnam. The ensuing siege ended seventy-seven days later in a tactical victory for the United States, which eventually abandoned the base, making it a heartbreaking and controversial symbol of American involvement in Vietnam. Bruce Clarke participated in the battle as a young U.S. Army officer, and his book combines his firsthand experiences and archival research to describe the saga of Khe Sanh.

$18.95 • Paperback • 6 x 9 • 208 pages • 11 b/w photos, 5 maps

Stackpole Military History Series

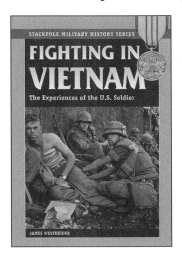

FIGHTING IN VIETNAM
THE EXPERIENCES OF THE U.S. SOLDIER
James Westheider

The Vietnam War differed from previous American wars of
the twentieth century. It was an undeclared and limited war
that divided the country and was fought disproportionately
by minorities and working-class whites, many of whom did
not want to serve. This is the story of the men and women
who participated in this generation-defining conflict overseas
and stateside—a war of search-and-destroy missions and
combat with an ill-defined enemy, but also a war of drug use,
fragging, and antiwar protests. With sweeping scope and
careful detail, James Westheider captures the many
dimensions of what it was like to fight in the Vietnam War.

$18.95 • Paperback • 6 x 9 • 256 pages • 32 b/w photos, 1 map

WWW.STACKPOLEBOOKS.COM
1-800-732-3669

Stackpole Military History Series

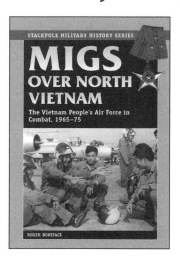

MIGS OVER NORTH VIETNAM
THE VIETNAM PEOPLE'S AIR FORCE IN COMBAT,
1965–75
Roger Boniface

Until now, the day-to-day operations of the Vietnam
People's Air Force have remained relatively unknown. In
MiGs over North Vietnam, Roger Boniface relies largely on
interviews with the participants to describe fighter
combat above Vietnam from 1965 to 1975, giving voice to
North Vietnamese pilots whose stories have never been
told, from deadly dogfights between MiGs and American
F-4s to persistent efforts to shoot down B-52 bombers.
This is the air war in Vietnam as seen by the other side.

*$18.95 • Paperback • 6 x 9 • 256 pages • 177 b/w photos, 6 maps,
26 color diagrams*

WWW.STACKPOLEBOOKS.COM
1-800-732-3669

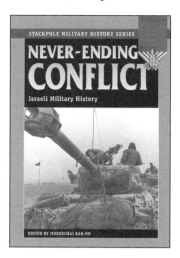

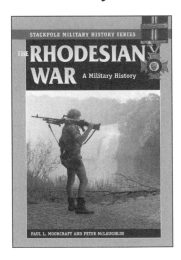

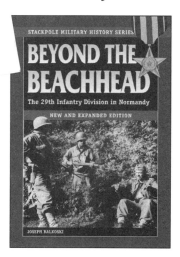

Stackpole Military History Series

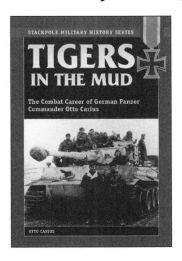

TIGERS IN THE MUD

THE COMBAT CAREER OF GERMAN PANZER COMMANDER OTTO CARIUS

Otto Carius,
translated by Robert J. Edwards

World War II began with a metallic roar as the
German Blitzkrieg raced across Europe, spearheaded
by the most dreadful weapon of the twentieth century:
the Panzer. Tank commander Otto Carius thrusts the
reader into the thick of battle, replete with the
blood, smoke, mud, and gunpowder so common
to the elite German fighting units.

$21.95 • Paperback • 6 x 9 • 368 pages
51 photos • 48 illustrations • 3 maps

WWW.STACKPOLEBOOKS.COM
1-800-732-3669

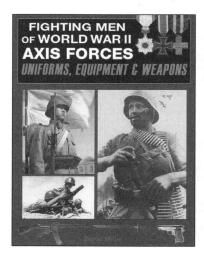
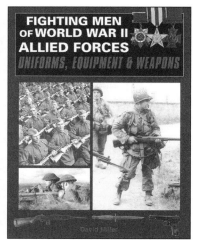